Divorce

London: The Stationery Office

First Published 2001

ISBN 0 11 702814 2

Disclaimer

Important note – please read this carefully

This book puts YOU in control. That is an excellent thing, but it also makes YOU responsible for using the book properly. Few washing machine manufacturers will honour their guarantee if you don't follow their 'instructions for use'. In the same way, we are unable to accept liability for any loss arising from mistakes or misunderstandings on your part. So please take time to read this book carefully.

This book is not a definitive statement of the law, although we believe it to be accurate as at 1 September 2001. We cannot accept liability for changes in the law that take place after the publication date, although every effort will be made to show any such changes on the website.

Contents

About the authors

Rosy Border has a First in French and has worked in publishing, lecturing and journalism as well as the law. She is a prolific author and adapter who stopped counting after 150 titles. Rosy and her husband, John Rabson, live in Suffolk and have a grown up family.

Jane Moir trained as a solicitor in Lincoln's Inn Fields, London. Since then she has practised extensively in family law. A member of the Solicitors' Family Law Association and a qualified mediator, she believes in 'Divorce with Dignity'. Jane is married to Andrew and her hobbies include hill walking, paragliding and teaching first aid.

Welcome

Welcome to the *You Need This Book First* series. Let's face it – the law is a maze. This book is your map through the part of the maze that deals with family law. It contains everything lawyers would tell you about this subject, if only they had time (and you had the money to pay them). And if you follow our advice you should be able to

- decide what course of action is for you
- jump through whatever legal hoops your course of action requires
- get your paperwork right
- understand *what* you are doing, and *why*.

Acknowledgements

A glance at the *Useful Contacts* section will show how many individuals and organisations we consulted while compiling this book. Thank you, everyone – especially John Rabson, Chartered Engineer, for his IT support, research and refreshments.

Introduction

We put YOU in control

This book empowers you. That is a good thing; but it means responsibility as well as power. Think of yourself as a driver using a road map. The map tells you the route, but you are in the driving seat.

Hazard signs

We warn you when you are in danger of getting out of your depth and need to take professional advice.

Watch out for the hazard sign.

Legal lore

Sometimes we pause to explain something: the origin of a word, perhaps, or why a particular piece of legislation was passed. You do not need to know these things to make use of this book, but we hope you find them interesting.

Power points

Sometimes we pause to empower you to do something.

Watch out for the symbol.

Clear English rules OK

Our prose style is WYSIWYG – *w*hat *y*ou *s*ee *i*s *w*hat *y*ou *g*et.

Legal documents have traditionally been written in archaic language, because this wording has stood the test of time – often several centuries – and has been hallowed by the courts. What is more, the use of technical language can sometimes enable specialists to express esoteric concepts in a kind of professional shorthand which is useful to them but meaningless to others.

The use of archaic language is, however, unnecessary and may be dangerous. The worst problem is that for non-specialists it is a foreign language, unknown at worst and incompletely understood at best, with all the potential for misunderstanding which that entails.

On the (fairly rare) occasions when we *do* need to use technical language, we offer clear explanations (see *Buzzwords* on page 5).

Click on our website

Check out our website, because buying this book gives you the right to use our exclusive readers' website.

www.youneedthisfirst.co.uk

Good luck – and drive carefully!

What this book can do for you

This book contains

- conciliation, separation or divorce? – exploring your options
- separation questionnaire – to help you to decide what to put in a separation agreement
- separation agreement – with clauses to suit individual cases
- the forms you need for a simple, uncontested divorce
- the forms you need to make arrangements for the children – by mutual agreement
- the advice you need to make financial arrangements – by mutual agreement.

Additionally, this book gives you

- general information that professional advisers would give you on the subject, if only they had the time to do so, and if only you had the money to pay them

- buzzwords that are important in this section of the law, and what they mean
- answers to some of the most frequently asked questions on the subject
- access to a website that is regularly updated.

What this book can't do for you

Make your decisions for you. We realise you and your partner will not be on the best of terms. We don't expect you to sit on the sofa and read this book together. All the same, it will take cooperation to make this book work. This is because you and your partner must *agree*

- whether to divorce; and if so
  - what type of divorce to apply for (see list on page 30)
  - what arrangements should be made for the children
  - who is to live where
  - what financial arrangements are to apply.

This book will not work for you otherwise. It does not provide the tools for

- a contested divorce
- disputes over children
- disputes over money.

If you envisage anything of the sort you will need a lawyer and quite a lot of money.

Buzzwords

Here are some words you will come across in this book. If they are already familiar to you, just skip this section.

Absent parent – also known as *non-resident parent* – the Child Support Agency's phrase for a parent who does not live with a child on the CSA's books (the parent the child lives with is called the *parent with care* – see below).

Acknowledgement of Service – thc form that the *Respondent* (see below) sends to the court to say he/she has received a divorce petition.

Affidavit – written evidence which replaces spoken evidence in court. An affidavit has to be sworn (see *Swear*, below). You will need an affidavit as evidence that the facts in your divorce petition are true.

Ancillary relief – the term lawyers use for the money and property side of divorce.

Legal lore

In Latin, an *ancilla* was a handmaiden; and anything ancillary would therefore be secondary, subsidiary, etc, to the main issue. Today it means maintenance payments, property adjustments and all the other financial aspects of family break-up. An aggrieved wife might claim *ancillary relief* if her husband shacked up with his own or someone else's handmaiden...

Answer – an official riposte to a divorce petition, usually defending oneself against what one sees as false accusations of unreasonable behaviour ('Oh no I didn't!' 'Oh yes you did!').

Annulment – the cancelling of a marriage as if it had never happened. This is exceptional but would apply, for example, in cases of bigamy.

Application for Directions for Trial – a formal request to the court saying that you want the case to go ahead.

Certificate of Entitlement to a Divorce – a paper signed by a judge, saying you have proved your point and setting a date for the *Decree Nisi* (see below) to be pronounced.

Certificate of Service – a document from the court confirming they have sent the divorce petition to the *Respondent* (see below).

Clean break – a court order (usually a *Consent order* – see below) which enables the two partners to walk away from the marriage without either having any further financial claim on the other. *Note*: a true clean break is *not* possible if there are dependent children.

Client care letter – the standard letter solicitors send each client explaining the terms under which they work, the hourly rate chargeable, who will handle the case and whom to approach in case of complaint.

Conciliation – sessions with an impartial third person to help couples to

- come to terms with the breakdown of their marriage
- reach an agreement (or reduce disagreement) in matters such as children, the matrimonial home, finance, etc.
- sort out arrangements for the future.

(see also *Mediation*, below).

Co-respondent – the third side of the eternal triangle.

Consent order – a court order in which both parties agree the financial arrangements (often, but not necessarily, a clean break – see above) and the judge rubber-stamps them to make them legally binding. *Consent* in this context means agreement.

Contact – 'visiting rights' for absent parents and their children. A *contact order* from a court requires the parent with whom the children lives to allow the child to visit, be visited by or stay with the absent parent.

County Court – the court that deals with divorce petitions. Cases are heard (lawspeak for considered) by judges. See also *Family Proceedings Court.*

Cross petition – a sort of tit-for-tat divorce petition, where X has filed for divorce against Y, who then files his or her own petition against X. Not surprisingly, the *Legal Services Commission* (see below) does not fund cross petitions and we don't advise them.

Decree – an order from the court. Judges can issue or *pronounce* decrees. See below.

Decree Absolute – the certificate that makes the divorce final and irreversible (except by remarrying your ex as Taylor and Burton did!).

Decree Nisi – a certificate that says you may have your divorce when you have served your time, which is six weeks and a day after the Decree Nisi. On (or after) that day the Petitioner can apply for the *Decree Absolute* (see above), which finalises the divorce.

Defended divorce – divorce proceedings in which one partner files a divorce petition but the other refuses to accept that the marriage is over and wants to stay married. This is different from *cross petitioning* (see above), where both parties accept that the marriage is over, but disagree about whose fault it is!

Directions – instructions from the court. A judge may call a *directions hearing*, eg, in disputes about children. During the hearing he will issue directions saying what is to happen next.

Disbursements – expenses; the money solicitors have to pay out on your behalf. A typical disbursement would be a court fee.

Legal lore

Disbursements is lawspeak for expenses: money paid out. It comes from old French *bourse*, a purse. And of course a *bursar* keeps a tight hold on the purse strings and a *bursary* is an award of money.

Divorce – the formal ending of a marriage, making a couple into two individuals.

Ex parte – without the other party being there. In family law, judges often make *injunctions* (see below) *ex parte* to protect wives from domestic violence. There is then a sort of return match *inter partes* a week or so later, when the other party attends court to tell their side of the story.

Legal lore

Lord Woolf is trying manfully to banish Latin and medieval French from the courts, but nobody has yet found a snappy translation for *ex parte*. 'One-sided' perhaps?

Family Proceedings Court – the Magistrates' Court, where cases are heard by magistrates (usually, but not always, non-lawyers with a qualified lawyer as clerk to the court).

File – pass or send to the court (first class post or delivery by hand is fine).

Ground(s) for divorce – a valid reason for granting a divorce on the basis that the marriage has broken down irretrievably.

Injunction – an order by a court for someone to do, or refrain from doing, something. In cases of domestic violence, the victim might apply for an injunction to restrain a violent partner.

Judicial separation – divorce in all but name. A Decree of Judicial Separation does not end the marriage but removes the couple's duty to live together.

Legal Help – free legal advice and assistance under the Legal Services Commission's scheme (formerly called the Green Form Scheme).

Legal Services Commission – formerly the Legal Aid Board: the body that provides public funding (formerly called Legal Aid) for people who meet certain strict financial criteria.

Litigant in person – someone representing him/herself in court, as opposed to instructing a lawyer. In a straightforward DIY divorce proceedings the two parties are litigants in person, but there is no need for them to attend court.

Lump sum order – a court order for one partner to pay the other a set sum, all in one chunk (often in lieu of continuing maintenance).

Maintenance pending suit – money to keep one partner going until they get their divorce and/or the details of their *ancillary relief* (see above) are finalised.

Matrimonial – to do with marriage. Lawyers often say *matrimonial* when most other people would say *family*. Wherever possible we prefer *family*, eg the *family* home.

Matrimonial home rights – also known as *rights of occupation* – the right to remain in the family home even if it is in your partner's sole name.

Mediation – help from an impartial third person to help couples considering separation or divorce to communicate better, to reduce conflict between them and to reach their own mutually agreed decisions about children, finances, property, etc. Mediation is not an attempt to salvage a marriage, although that may sometimes happen, but rather a sort of damage limitation exercise to help couples to end their relationship amicably.

Parent with care (of a child) – the Child Support Agency's phrase for the parent with whom a child lives (as opposed to the *absent parent*, above).

Parental responsibility – a catch-all phrase relating to the duties, powers and rights of a parent in relation to a child.

Party – lawspeak for a person involved in a court case, which gives rise to gems like 'parity of the party of the first part with the party of the second part'.

Periodical payments – weekly or monthly (maintenance) payments.

Petition – an application for a divorce; *petitioning* is applying for a divorce and the *petitioner* is the partner asking for a divorce.

Prayer – a request to the court to grant a divorce and any other associated things (eg fees, periodic payments, lump sums, property adjustment orders, etc).

Privileged – confidential. Anything said or written that is 'privileged' may only be reported to the court if everyone involved in the discussions or correspondence agrees to this.

Prohibited steps order – an order of the court to prevent something from happening without the Court's consent, such as taking a child out of the country.

Property adjustment order – a court order saying who is to have what property, eg the family home.

Public Funding – formerly Legal Aid – means-tested legal assistance from the *Legal Services Commission* (see above).

Residence order – an order from the court, concerning where a child is to live, and with whom. *Residence* has replaced 'custody', with its implications of 'remanded in ...', and a good thing too.

Respondent – the other party: the counterpart to the *Petitioner* (see above). A handy memory aid is 'the petitioner applies and the respondent replies'.

Secured periodical payments – payments that are secured in some way, such as with a charge (like a mortgage) on the payer's house.

Serve – send or hand a document to the other party in a case and be able to prove you have done so (see *Certificate of Service*, above).

Specific issue order – an order of the court about a particular question which has arisen in relation to a child, and on which the parents disagree. This may concern religion, health, etc.

Statement of Arrangements for Children – the form enclosed with a divorce petition, which sets out the arrangements for the children: where they will live and with whom, and what contact they will have with the absent parent.

Statutory Charge – money the Legal Services Commission claws back to pay its fees. See page 81 for a full explanation.

Suit – a fancy name for case (out of the same stable as 'sue').

Swear – say on oath, in the presence of a solicitor or an officer of the court, that a statement is true.

Frequently asked questions

I have been married just six months and it has been a disaster. How soon can I get a divorce?

You cannot file for divorce until you have been married for a year. You can, of course, separate at once, and if you are really miserable together this may be the wisest course of action.

I would like some general advice on divorce. I recall my sister getting an interview for a fixed £5 fee. Does this still apply?

No. The scheme was abolished in 1993 and has not been replaced. But many solicitors offer fixed-fee interviews, although the fee is usually considerably more than £5. Some even offer 15 minutes free of charge. Ask around.

My friend's marriage break-up cost a fortune in legal fees. Can I get a divorce without using a solicitor?

Yes – provided everything is straightforward and non-contentious. We show you how to do it for just the court fees, which are currently £180 (£150 to issue proceedings and £30 to make the decree absolute).

Most court staff are helpful and may even glance over your paperwork to make sure nothing is missing. But divorce itself is only part of the story. It is likely that the bulk of your friend's legal costs involved the financial side of the break-up. This is why it is better to try to agree a rough, ball park financial arrangement before you consult solicitors, who can then fine-tune it and get it 'blessed' by the court.

I want a divorce, but I can't find our marriage certificate. What can I do?

Send for a copy from the local registrar of births, deaths and marriages, which will cost you £6.50 and take about two weeks. If you want it urgently they can get a copy out to you by the next working day for £22. A second option is to apply to the central General Register Office – see the address on page 218 – which will cost you £11, or £27 if you wish them to send it to you within two working days.

If you were married abroad and the marriage certificate is not in English, you will have to get it translated and the translation notarised, ie sworn to be accurate. Look up *Translators* in *Yellow Pages*.

My wife is applying for a divorce. Will I have to go to court?

Not for a straightforward divorce. The judge will go through the paperwork and will, if all is correct, grant her a Decree Nisi. Disputes over money, children, etc, later, are a different matter: couples who cannot agree such things may end up asking a judge to decide, and this could involve appearing in court.

My home is in the UK, but I spend a lot of time working abroad. Can I get a divorce in the UK?

Yes, if the UK is your permanent home and if you got married in the UK. But if in doubt seek professional advice.

I have married someone who I now know was married already. Can I get a divorce?

You don't need a divorce, because your marriage is 'void' – invalid; you have never been legally married. Technically, you were never married at all. However, it is wise to get a court order to annul the 'marriage', as you can then apply to the court for ancillary relief (see *Buzzwords*); also, your status will then be clear if you ever wish to marry 'properly'. Seek legal advice.

I have heard about 'quickie divorces'. Can I get one – and how quick are they?

(a) yes, possibly – see below; and

(b) how long is a piece of string?

A 'no-fault' divorce by mutual consent, where neither party blames the other, would require two years' separation. To obtain a divorce in under two years one of you would have to say that the other was guilty either of adultery or of unreasonable behaviour. In both instances, therefore, one of you will have to blame the other, with all the accompanying hurt and anger. After that, it will depend on how busy your local court is, how prompt each party is in turning around the paperwork and how speedily you can finalise your financial and other arrangements. There is, in any case, a built-in waiting period of six weeks between the petitioner being granted a Decree Nisi and being allowed to apply for the decree to be made absolute. Three months, with a following wind, would be an absolute minimum.

Why this emphasis on speed? Legislation was passed in 1996 – but at the time of writing has not yet come fully into force – to impose 'a period of time for reflection and consideration in order for the couple to address what has gone wrong in the marriage, whether there is any hope of reconciliation and, in the event that the breakdown is irretrievable, to make proper arrangements for living apart once a divorce order is made'. (*Looking to the Future: Mediation and the Ground for Divorce* (CM 2799) April 1995.) Is that such a bad thing?

Do I need to name the co-respondent in my adultery petition? I don't really blame her and I don't want to make her any more miserable than my husband has already.

No, you need not name her (see page 103). Naming the co-respondent in an adultery petition can be quite a spiteful thing to do, because divorce papers are served on the co-respondent as well as on the respondent. Quite apart from whether being spiteful is good for your soul, you might well spare your children, and the co-respondent's children too, a lot of unhappiness, and even get a quicker financial settlement if you can keep the emotional temperature down.

We have agreed between ourselves where the children are to live, and arranged 'visiting rights'. Do we need to go to court to confirm this?

No. Whichever of you is the petitioner will file a Statement of Arrangements for Children with the divorce petition, and the judge will take this into account when deciding whether to grant a divorce. Unless you have proposed something outrageous or missed out something vital (it happens!), the Statement of Arrangements should be 'blessed' by the judge without anyone having to go to court.

Is there any way I can get my husband to pay maintenance for me and our child before our divorce is finalised?

Yes. You can apply to the court for *maintenance pending suit* (see *Buzzwords*), for which you will need professional advice. It is better and less expensive, of course, to agree something between you. Sit down with the figures and sort it out.

I am on Income Support and cannot afford the court fees. Will this stop me getting a divorce?

No. There is a special form to apply for remission of court fees. There is an example on pages 190–192, and one can be downloaded from our website.

—Moreover, if you are on Income Support (or one of several other kinds of benefit), you will almost certainly qualify for free professional advice and assistance too. Choose a solicitor who holds a Legal Services Commission franchise; you should not have to pay anything at all because the LSC pays your fees for you. See the *Legal Help and Public Funding* on page 77.

—I shall be on Income Support after my divorce and my husband has not yet told me how much maintenance he will be paying for our children. Who can advise?

The Child Support Agency will automatically become involved, because you are on State benefits. The CSA will assess your ex's income and outgoings and set a figure for maintenance payments. Your own welfare benefits will be adjusted accordingly. Some people say the CSA should be renamed Treasury Support Agency because that's where your ex's maintenance payments will go!

—Our family home is in my partner's sole name and he is threatening to kick me out. Can he do this?

No. You have 'rights of occupation' (or 'matrimonial home rights') until the fate of the property is decided (i.e. after your divorce proceedings) and, provided you stay put, your partner cannot evict you without a court order. Moreover, you can prevent your partner from selling the home without your knowledge. See *The Family Home* on page 123.

My wife and I have lived apart for many years without any problems; but I would now like to remarry. My wife, however, does not want a divorce. What can I do?

If you have been separated for at least five years you can get a divorce without your wife's agreement (see page 90).

Exploring your options

A troubled marriage

Marriages can get into trouble for a variety of reasons. Sometimes you can grit your teeth and press on in the hope that you are just going through a bad patch and that things will get better. Often they do; every marriage has peaks, troughs and plateaux.

Sharing your troubles with friends who have survived similar experiences can be helpful. But you may reach the point where you need to explore other options

- conciliation and counselling
- separation
- divorce.

You need to be aware of the implications of your choice on

- your children
- your finances
- your home.

We explore the options with you. But first of all –

It needn't be anybody's fault!

There is far less talk about guilty and innocent parties than there used to be. The courts are not in the retribution business. They are not interested in punishing anybody for bad behaviour or rewarding anyone for virtue. If, after examining all the options, you do decide to seek a divorce, you will find that the courts are far more interested in protecting the vulnerable – especially children – than in blaming either partner for the break-up of the marriage. For the sake of those same children, not to mention your family and friends, it is important to settle everything as calmly as possible.

Can we work it out? Talking it over

If you and your partner are still on speaking terms, it may be worth trying to resolve your differences yourselves. Meeting on neutral ground with a written agenda like a business meeting is one strategy which some couples find helpful, but it takes a lot of goodwill on both sides, and without a third person to referee the discussion there is a danger that the more forceful partner will have all their own way.

If you find it difficult to talk out your problems without one or other of you getting bulldozed, or the discussion degenerating into a screaming match, you should consider getting in a mediator.

Couples in trouble have a wide choice of skilled help to help them to make sense of their problems – money, the family home, business issues, debts and, not least, the children – and steer them towards a solution without incurring crippling legal costs.

One of the key aims of the Family Law Act 1996 (which at the time of writing has not yet fully come into force, although it is already influencing the thinking both of professionals and of the Legal Services Commission – see *Buzzwords*), is to persuade couples to seek conciliation and/or mediation before starting divorce proceedings.

Conciliation and counselling

Forget words such as *conciliatory*, with undertones of appeasement, placation and sucking-up. *Conciliation* in this context simply means getting a third person, usually a trained counsellor, to help you to resolve your problems for yourselves.

The difficulty with conciliation or marriage guidance counselling is that it takes time to set it up, and you may need (or believe you need) help at once. There may, according to local needs and conditions, be a waiting list of several months to see a Relate counsellor. We know couples who, by the time their appointment with Relate came up, had decided to give their marriage another chance.

You may face a long or inconvenient trip to your nearest counsellor. Provision is not uniform; much depends on where you live, and the nearest counsellor may be many miles away, with only minimal public transport available. Couples without a car are really penalised here.

Even so, conciliation is always worth considering, and worth any amount of inconvenience if it works for you. Clearly, if your husband has just come home roaring drunk and knocked you about (and if he has, you should turn to *Emergencies* on page 72 NOW!), an appointment with a counsellor in three weeks' time is not much help. But in general it is unwise to decide that your relationship is damaged beyond repair, without giving conciliation a chance.

Possibilities for consideration are

- 'Relate' (see your local telephone directory)
- local organisations such as (in Suffolk) PACT (Parents' Conciliation Trust), which specialises in looking after the needs of the children. Check with your local Citizens' Advice Bureau for details
- some doctors' surgeries can refer patients to independent counsellors; ask around
- Look on notice boards in your public library, or call the Citizens' Advice Bureau, to see what is available locally; and check out *Useful Contacts* on page 218.

Mediation

Many couples agree to call in a third person, called a mediator, to help them to resolve areas of disagreement or dispute. There are big advantages over slugging it out between solicitors, not least the saving in cost.

Mediators are impartial. They have no authority to make any decisions about your dispute(s). A mediator will help you to reach a decision, resolving your disagreements by negotiation.

Mediation is not the same as counselling. Counselling is about feelings; and a mediator may suggest you see a counsellor if they think you need help in understanding and handling your feelings.

Counselling is intended to help partners to stay together. Mediation accepts that some relationships do break down, and if yours is one of these, the mediator will help you sort out your practical and legal arrangements for the future.

Mediation can be used at any stage, whether you are trying to stay together or whether you are in the final stages of divorce. It is mentioned here only because you need to be aware of it: you might decide to try it at a much later stage – for example, to resolve a dispute over financial matters – and that would be quite in order.

Mediation sessions are private and quite informal. You will normally need between two and four sessions of about 90 minutes.

Mediation can help you sort out:

- arrangements for your children
- dividing up your property
- financial details

and any other practical issues associated with your separation or divorce.

If mediation is being used to discuss arrangements for your children, the mediator will expect you to consider the children's needs and wishes first.

If mediation is being used to deal with property or financial arrangements, the mediator will ask you both to fill in a form giving full details of your property, loans, debts, income, outgoings and any other relevant information. An example of this form is reproduced on page 154 because you will probably find it helpful in sorting out your finances, whether or not you decide to go for mediation.

This factual information may be used later in court to help with any financial arrangements; it is, however, the only information that will be passed on. Anything that either of you says during the sessions is privileged and the mediator will not divulge it unless you both give your permission – with one exception. *If the mediator considers that any child or adult has suffered significant harm or is at risk of being harmed, then the mediator will inform the police or social services.*

All mediators are specially qualified. Many are solicitors who have also taken a further course in mediation. Others are members of the UK College of Family Mediators.

There is no fixed fee for mediation: different mediators charge different rates. But if you are on a low income you may not have to pay anything.

Mediators have a duty to ensure that all sessions are conducted fairly and that both parties feel safe. Mediators are impartial. They are not adjudicators, and they are not advocates either; they do not judge and they do not take sides.

We repeat: mediators have no authority to make any decisions regarding your disputes. Their job is to help you to resolve your disagreements yourselves, by negotiation.

When is mediation NOT the answer?

Mediation is not the answer:

- when someone is less than frank and honest

For mediation to work successfully, both partners must be frank with each other.

- when someone feels unsafe or intimidated

Neither partner should feel threatened or pressurised by the other.

- when the dispute is something you cannot be expected to resolve for yourselves
- if either of you lacks the mental capacity to take part in mediation
- where there is violent behaviour on the part of one (or both) of you
- where emergency proceedings have to be taken, such as child protection issues or violence within the family
- where there is a court order banning one partner from having contact with the other
- in financial disputes where either of you is bankrupt
- in certain matters where only the court can decide, such as in cases involving the paternity of a child
- where marital therapy or counselling would be more helpful.

However, there is a lot to be said for mediation:

- it helps you to find a solution that both partners feel is fair. There will not be any winner or loser. Instead, mediation is intended to help you to reach sensible, practical arrangements
- it can help to reduce animosity and misunderstandings between the two partners
- mediation improves communication between partners, which is particularly important if you have children.

I want out – what can I do?

Well, you could separate ...

Reasons for separating

Suppose you and your partner have decided you can no longer bear to live together. Here are four possible reasons for finding life as a couple intolerable:

- you are miserable together
- you want time out in the hope of saving your marriage
- someone is at risk if you stay together (if this is you, turn at once to *Emergencies* on page 72)
- you have decided you may want a divorce on the grounds of separation (see below) rather than one of the other 'reasons'.

'Reasons' for divorce

To qualify for a divorce, you must show that the marriage has broken down irretrievably. The court recognises five 'reasons' for this irretrievable breakdown. Before considering your options, let's look at these 'reasons' for a court to grant a divorce, because they will influence any decision you make about separation. Here are all five, although in practice the fifth seldom arises nowadays.

1. your partner has committed adultery and you find it unbearable to continue living with them
2. your partner has behaved unreasonably, to such an extent that you find it unbearable to continue living with them
3. you and your partner have lived apart for two years and you both agree to a divorce
4. you and your partner have lived apart for five years – one of you can obtain a divorce without the other's agreement
5. your partner has deserted you.

Reasons 1 and 2 would enable you to apply for a divorce without a period of separation. The tabloid newspapers sometimes refer to such divorces as quickie divorces because wronged spouses can file for one immediately, without a compulsory separation period. If one of you is in a hurry to marry someone else, 1 or 2 would be the reasons to consider, provided you did not mind blaming the marriage breakdown on your partner and provided they did not mind being blamed. We'll come back to those in more detail later.

To qualify for reason 3 or 4, you would need to live apart for the qualifying period. So you would separate, and mark the date of separation in your respective diaries.

Legal lore

Judicial separation?

Some couples say, 'We're having a judicial separation'. Most are mistaken. A judicial separation isn't just any old separation. It is a separation which has been 'blessed' by a court.

Some cultures and religions frown on divorce, even in the face of adultery or cruelty. In those circumstances, couples separate permanently in preference to obtaining a divorce. A Decree of Judicial Separation does not require the agreement of the other partner. The procedure is the same as for a divorce (see the flowchart on page 85), but without the final split.

Judicial separation is not common. There are many cases, however, when separation is *judicious* – a wise or prudent thing to do; and you won't need a court order to do it.

Under one roof?

Let us suppose that you decide to separate, either to give yourselves time out from a difficult relationship or as a basis for a divorce by mutual agreement in two years' time.

If your house is big enough, or if you could work out a rota to use the kitchen and bathroom, you could in theory live separate lives under one roof. In practice it can be quite difficult, but it does have three very big advantages:

- it gives you time to sort out your financial affairs and arrangements concerning housing, including keeping any mortgage payments going
- there is less disruption for any children
- it is bound to be cheaper than maintaining separate households.

The down side of this arrangement is that it may be difficult to prove to a court that you have in fact lived separate lives under the same roof. You will need to convince the judge that you have

- slept in separate bedrooms
- cooked separate meals and eaten them apart
- each done your own household chores
- each done your own shopping
- had your washing done separately
- behaved like two strangers living under the same roof.

Legal lore

In a famous case, *Mouncer and Mouncer*, the judge refused to grant Mr and Mrs Mouncer a divorce because during their separation there had been a certain amount of family life – shared meals, etc. – going on.

'Separate lives' means just that. It could be a fairly joyless existence, and you might even decide you would be happier living together after all.

Splitting up is rarely simple

Even without the complications of trying to live separate lives under one roof, many couples, after they have looked carefully at the implications of separating, decide to give their relationship another chance.

The legal process of breaking up is straightforward – *provided you are childless, homeless and penniless.* Such people can simply walk away from each other and stop living together. For anyone else, there are many things to consider. The more children, property and money you and your partner have, the more you have to think about before you separate.

First, any children of the family have to be considered:

- Who will they live with?
- Who will support them?
- What contact will the other parent have with them?

Second, there is the property and financial side:

- What will happen to the family home?
- What will each partner live on?
- How will any assets be divided?
- What about pension rights?

All these are problems that you must deal with, whether you are divorcing or only separating.

Apart – but still married

If you live apart but are still married:

- separation is quick – in an emergency it can be instant
- you can separate without going to court
- separation is reversible – you are still married and can get together again at any time.

Separation, however you go about it, keeps the marriage in existence even if your relationship has died. *You are still legally married.*

The up side of still being married is of course that you can get together again at any time. Meanwhile you can use the time apart to think carefully about the future. If you decide to get together again, you can start afresh as if nothing had happened. That is a lot easier (not to mention cheaper) than emulating Elizabeth Taylor and Richard Burton and divorcing, only to remarry later.

Even if you are sure that no amount of time and space can change your mind, living apart for a while before you start divorce proceedings can help to reduce the bitterness and make the eventual divorce less painful for everyone.

It is probably fair to say that there is a period of separation – physical or emotional – before every divorce. We know of couples who (almost) enjoyed their separation. They would meet once a week to do the shopping together and use this time to discuss any domestic details such as the children's school arrangements. The husband would come for supper once a week and afterwards do any small DIY chores around the house while his wife did his ironing. By the time they eventually filed for divorce they had sorted everything out amicably – and it did not cost them a penny in legal fees.

The down side of still being married is that *in the eyes of the law you are still a couple*. So, unless you change your will, your partner will inherit your estate when you die. You will also need to think about the future of the family home. See more about this on page 123.

Separation without agreement

Separation without agreement can mean

- one partner walking out
- one partner kicking the other out
- police and/or courts stepping in to remove one partner for the protection of the other and/or the children.

These kinds of separation are drastic and can be instant. A court can order one partner out of the family home. Orders are available in the Magistrates' Court and County Court to protect vulnerable people from violence and harassment. If you need one of these, it is probably an emergency (see *Emergencies* on page 72).

Separation with agreement

Suppose that your partner is sensible and you believe the two of you can work something out and abide by it. You might decide to separate by agreement.

This may be

- an informal agreement
- a formal agreement.

We explain both below. The distinction between an informal and a formal agreement is ours, and as such has no force in law.

Any agreement is pointless unless there is a good chance of both partners sticking to it. Don't bother seeking an agreement of any kind if your partner is

- violent
- a danger to you or to the children
- thoroughly untrustworthy.

You may need a court order (see below) to make them behave.

Informal agreement

You have talked things over. You may also have exchanged letters, setting out what you have decided. There is no formal document, and you probably did not take legal advice, but you have worked out an arrangement and hope to stick to it.

For:

- you sort everything out to suit your own needs
- it does not cost you any money
- nobody else is involved. You did it your way.

Against:

- you may regard your agreement as binding, but the court may not
- if either partner breaks a promise, it is hard to make them toe the line
- you might not get it right; the agreement might not do what you meant it to.

Formal written agreement

You have talked things over. You may also have exchanged letters setting out what you have decided. You then set out what you have agreed in a written agreement, probably based on the sample agreement at the back of this book, and you both sign and date it.

If you eventually divorce, you can use the financial and property aspects of your agreement as the basis for a legally binding *consent order* (see *Buzzwords*) which will be 'blessed' by the court.

For:

- you sort everything out to suit your own needs
- the cost is minimal

- it is easier to enforce than an informal agreement
- courts will be more likely to accept it
- everything is properly set out: you know where you stand
- if you decide on a divorce later, two years' separation will provide grounds for one, with no hard feelings
- it isn't nearly as final as divorce!

Against:

- courts can still overturn a separation agreement dealing with financial matters
- the Child Support Agency can change child maintenance payments even if you are both happy with them
- neither of you will be able to petition for divorce on grounds of desertion (note, however, that very few people do anyway).

Ending a separation agreement

Typically, a separation agreement is ended by

- divorce
- the death of either partner
- both partners deciding to end the agreement, for whatever reason
- the couple getting together again.

What should a separation agreement cover?

Whether formal or informal, any separation agreement will need to cover the things you would have to work out if you were planning to divorce. These are, basically,

- property
- money, and
- children

but not necessarily in that order. See the draft separation agreement on page 55. Even if you decide to do things informally, it is worth using this example as a sort of agenda of points to take into account.

Of course, every situation is unique and you may need to adapt our agreement to suit your own circumstances. We show you how to go about this.

The following are some points to consider.

Dividing the assets

Separation seriously harms your wealth. Keeping up two households is bound to cost more than one.

You will have to make a list of everything you own, individually and jointly, and decide who needs what.

- suppose you own the family home jointly, with a mortgage:
  - Who will live there?
  - Who will pay the mortgage?
  - Will one of you buy the other out? (see also *Housing*, below).
- What will happen to joint bank and building society accounts?
- What about pensions?
- Who will service any debts and/or HP?
- Suppose you have a family car:
  - Will you sell it and divide the proceeds?
  - Or will the car go to the partner who needs transport for work or the school run?
- What about furniture and other household items?

Consider too, what will happen if one of you dies? Remember that if you die without making a will, by law your partner will inherit all or a large chunk of your estate whether you are on good terms or not. Find out more about this in our book on wills, *Write Your Own Will*, in this series.

Housing

- Who will live where? And who will pay the rent or mortgage?

- Can one of you claim Housing Benefit (to help pay for rented accommodation) or Income Support (to help with mortgage payments)?

Maintenance

- For your partner
- For your children.

Even if you don't think you need any maintenance, or if your partner is refusing to ask for any, put a nominal sum – even 5p a year – in any separation agreement you make. Why bother? Because if your circumstances change, you can then go to court and get your maintenance allowance increased. If you don't put in any maintenance arrangements, you could find it hard to persuade a court to order any maintenance later on.

- Always allow for change – suppose one of you loses their job, retires, dies or even comes into a fortune?
- Remember that the Child Support Agency (see page 46) can in certain circumstances override any agreement regarding maintenance for children.

Benefits

If you and your partner separate or divorce, there may not be enough money to go round. You may need to consider getting benefits to help you manage financially, especially if your partner is refusing to keep up payments on which you used to rely before your separation.

The *Useful Contacts* section on page 218 directs you to a government website that lists benefits you may never have known existed. Here, however, are some of the main benefits. And remember that the estranged partner of a rich person is classed as single and may thus qualify for benefits if they have little money of their own.

Job Seeker's Allowance is an option if you are able to work but are either not working or working on average less than 16 hours per week.

If you have children you may also be entitled to *Child Benefit*.

People are only entitled to *Income Support* if they are on a low income and have savings under a certain amount (usually £8,000 but not always), are over the age of 16 and are not working, or on average work less than 16 hours per week.

Anybody who is on a low income and paying rent can claim *Housing Benefit* and *Council Tax Benefit*. If you have children and their other parent is living elsewhere, you may also claim *Child Support Maintenance*.

You may qualify for an *emergency loan*, eg for basic furnishings or removal costs if you move out of the family home.

If you apply for benefits, the DSS will automatically send your partner a Child Support Agency form. It takes the view that it is better for an absent parent to support the children than the state.

Children

We are talking about people, not possessions, here. It has always been self-evident that the children's needs must come first; and in the 1989 Children Act this is spelled out by the law: the word the Act uses is *paramount.*

Keep the heat down!

Your children love you both and they will find it hard to understand why you don't seem to love each other any more. Any arrangements you make must disregard your own hurt feelings and concentrate on causing the children as little damage or upheaval as possible.

Some don'ts

You may feel tempted to use a sympathetic child as a confidant – don't.

Don't, under any circumstances, discuss the details of your marriage breakdown with your children. And *don't* try to persuade them that the break-up is all your partner's fault EVEN IF YOU ARE QUITE SURE THAT IT IS TRUE.

Don't let young children see your bitterness towards your partner. Children become very confused if one parent shows feelings of hatred or disgust for the other.

Don't let your children take sides.

Your children need to keep their love and respect for both parents, and this will become more and more important to them, and to you, as time goes on. In worst-case scenarios, where children are drawn into their parents' disputes, they can be scarred emotionally, which can lead to behavioural problems. Their education is likely to suffer too, as any experienced teacher will tell you. To learn and develop and grow into happy, well-adjusted adults, children need a happy and secure environment.

It is probably very difficult for you to protect your children from the emotional warfare that is going on around them, especially if your partner seems hell-bent on breaking all the rules; but protect them you must. So keep the heat down!

This subject is returned to on page 138 but no apology is made for introducing it here.

Arrangements for children

Here are some typical questions to ask yourselves.

- Who will the children live with?
  - During the week?
  - At weekends?
- Maintenance – who will pay the bills?
- Contact

  - What arrangements will there be for the absent parent to see them?
  - Can grandparents and other relations keep in touch too?
- Is there anything extra, such as school fees or hospital appointments, that might need to be dealt with in your case?

Even if you have no immediate plans for divorce, it is worth looking at the *Statement of Arrangements for Children*, see page 107. This is a form that tells the court what arrangements will be made for the children when the couple split up, and it is very comprehensive. Use the questions in the form as guidelines for your discussions.

The Child Support Agency

Since April 1993 child maintenance has been the responsibility of the Child Support Agency (CSA), with the job of trying to get absent parents (usually fathers, but not always) to maintain their children according to the CSA's assessment of the absent parent's means.

The CSA provides two helplines and a website – see *Useful contacts* on page 218 – and has branches in main DSS offices.

It has had a very bad press, and an alarming percentage of its assessments seem to have been inaccurate, but its aim is a praiseworthy one: to shift responsibility for child maintenance from the state to the absent parent.

When does the CSA get involved?

The CSA gets involved:

- always if the DSS is concerned in the case, for example if one partner is claiming Income Support
- if you cannot agree the amount of maintenance and one of you asks the CSA for an assessment
- if someone blows the whistle – for example, if a couple has had a child maintenance agreement that has broken down.

When does the CSA *not* get involved?

In general, if no public money is involved and nobody complains. The court has no power to intervene in cases where there is still a dispute about maintenance. However, it is possible for people involved in divorce proceedings or judicial separation (see page 32) to bypass the CSA by written agreement. It would not, however, be a DIY matter. You would need to seek professional advice.

The present arrangements

At the time of writing, the Child Support Agency works out the amount of maintenance payable using a complex formula. The formula takes into account the income of both parents unless the parent with care (see *Buzzwords*) receives Income Support, Job Seeker's Allowance or Working Families Tax Credit.

If you are not getting Income Support or Job Seeker's Allowance and cannot reach an agreement about maintenance with your spouse, you can still use the Child Support Agency if the following apply to you:

- there is no existing maintenance order concerning the child or children
- the child or children are under 16 years of age, or if they are over 16 years they are still in full-time secondary education
- your partner is not living in the same household as the child or children; and you live in the UK
- finally, and perhaps most importantly, the child is the child by birth or adoption of both yourself and your spouse. Stepchildren cannot get support from their step-parents under the Child Support Agency.

The Child Support Agency can unfortunately take a very long time to process applications. Applications are meant to be processed by the CSA within 20 weeks, but they usually take longer.

Payments assessed by the Child Support Agency cannot exceed 30% of the paying parent's income after tax, National Insurance, their reasonable housing costs and 50% of their pension contributions have been deducted from their income. A further deduction is made if they have any new children of their own. The amount of Child Support is also dependent upon the number of nights that the children spend with you. For example, if the children spent approximately half the year with the other parent then the amount payable under the Child

Support Agency assessment would be drastically reduced.

Legal lore

Child support legislation was recently changed by the Child Support, Pensions and Social Security Act 2000, which will apply a new formula to child support from 2002. At the time of going to press these arrangements are not yet in force, but full details should be available either from the CSA or from local DSS offices.

Will you qualify for Legal Help?

Community Legal Service

The bad news. Breaking up, as we said before, should carry a wealth warning. Most vulnerable are wives with little or no money of their own.

The good news. A person who is separated from his or her partner is considered as a single person. So even a rich man's wife, if she has little money of her own, may well qualify for Legal Help. Does this mean YOU? See *Legal Help and Public Funding* on page 77.

Your separation questionnaire

This questionnaire will help you to draft your separation agreement. Some of the information will also be needed if you later decide to apply for a divorce.

First, the easy bits:

Your name..

Your partner's name...

The address where **you** will be living

....

....

The address where **your partner** will be living

....

....

Children: names and dates of birth

1. ....DOB

2. ....DOB

3. ....DOB

4. ....DOB

5. ....DOB

6. ....DOB

(include any stepchildren, etc)

Details of where each child will be living

1. ....

2 ....

3. ....

4. ....

5. ....

6. ....

Dates

The date and place you and your partner married

....

The date and place you and your partner last lived together

....

Housing

Will you remain in the family home?

Yes

Is the rent or mortgage being paid?

Yes – Fine, but don't be complacent. Tell your council, housing association, landlord or building society what has happened and ask to be notified if your partner stops paying.

No – Tell your council, housing association, landlord or building society NOW and ask for advice.

Can you afford to pay the rent/mortgage yourself?

Yes – Fine, but try to get your partner to contribute, especially if there are children involved.

No – If your partner cannot or will not contribute, ask about Housing Benefit/Income Support (see *Useful Contacts* on page 218). Ask the building society to let you make lower repayments until you sort yourself out.

Meanwhile, try to get your partner to pay. You may qualify for Legal Help to do this. See *Legal Help and Public Funding* on page 77.

No

Have you got somewhere else to live?

Yes – Fine. Remember that you may qualify for Housing Benefit even for private rentals.

No – tell the council or housing association NOW and ask for advice. Provision varies, so it is not possible to generalise.

If one of you leaves the family home, they need to tell

- the building society or bank (ie the mortgage lender), if your home is mortgaged
- the landlord if you live in private rented accommodation
- the council or housing association if you live in council or housing association property.

They need to know, and your partner may not bother to inform them. It is also a good idea to tell

- the local council with regard to Council Tax (the one left behind may qualify for Council Tax relief)
- water supplier
- electricity supplier
- gas supplier.

It is sensible to do this yourself in case your partner forgets – or deliberately neglects – this chore.

Protecting the family home

People can do strange things if they are under a lot of stress, and marriage break-up is one of the most stressful things that can happen to you. So we will mention here the importance of protecting your stake in the family home to make sure your partner does not dispose of it while your back is turned! Even if the family home is owned – or rented – the principle is the same – in your partner's sole name, you have 'rights of occupation' (or 'matrimonial home rights' – both terms are in current use) and you can also make sure they do not sell or otherwise dispose of it without your permission. We tell you how to do this – see page 123.

Money

Can you afford to keep yourself (and the children)?

Yes – Fine, but your partner has responsibilities. Try to get your partner to contribute – especially if there are children. Consider contacting the Child Support Agency – see *Useful Contacts* on page 218 for an unofficial assessment of how much they should be paying.

No – ask about Income Support, or Working Family Tax Credit if you are working. See *Useful Contacts* on page 218.

You may also qualify for an emergency loan to help, for example, with the cost of moving house. Note that if you have children, and if you apply for benefits, the DSS will automatically send a Child Support Agency form. It takes the view that it is better for an absent parent to support the children than the state.

Have you a joint bank or building society account?

Yes – Quick! – make sure your partner can't draw out all the money (consider getting there first!). Or ask the bank not to honour any transactions unless both of you have signed.

No – Lucky you! But check any other joint assets to make sure your partner can't dispose of those. See *Protecting the family home*, above.

What about the family car? Consider putting the vehicle registration document in a *very* safe place until the future of the car has been decided.

Have you a bank or building society account of your own?

Yes – Congratulations. You are going to need it.

No – Open one NOW.

Draft separation agreement

Here is a draft separation agreement. It is not exhaustive. You would certainly need to change some items to suit your own circumstances.

We recommend that you write down the main points that you have agreed with your partner, probably using the questionnaire on page 50 as a starting point. Make sure you really have reached an agreement and that there are no misunderstandings. Make sure that you have all your financial information together (you may like to use the financial form on page 154 as a guide), and that you have been frank with each other about your assets. If it comes to court proceedings later, you will both have to disclose all your financial affairs, and openness now could save a lot of unpleasantness later.

Spend time now, save money later

If in the future you need to instruct a solicitor about the financial side of your marriage break-up (and you will almost certainly need one if your affairs are at all complicated), any work you put in now is likely to reduce the amount of time your solicitor needs to spend on your case. Your solicitor will be able to use the information in this draft separation agreement when, for example, it is time to draw up a consent order.

Remember that lawyers charge mainly on the basis of time spent; so anything that makes it easier, and therefore quicker, for them to handle your case will automatically save you money.

In the meantime, the separation agreement below, although not legally binding, addresses all the issues that are likely to arise. We have provided for the agreement to be witnessed, to impress upon you and your partner that although it might not stand up in a court of law, you are meant to stick to it. If you are both sincere about this, it should be sufficient to tide you over until

- you actually divorce, or
- you decide to live together again.

Note that the agreement automatically comes to an end if

- one of you dies
- you resume living together
- any court order is made to cancel or vary the terms of the agreement, or
- both of you agree in writing to end or vary the agreement.

Separation agreement

(Note that we have called you Partner 1 and Partner 2. When you come to 'personalise' your agreement, please replace P1 and P2 with your forenames.)

THIS SEPARATION AGREEMENT is made the .... day of .... 200[ ]

between:
Partner 1:..of

[address]...

....

and:
Partner 2:..of

[address]...

....

Background

1. [Partner 1] and [Partner 2]

were married on .... [date] at [place] [Copy this from the marriage certificate. It has to be absolutely correct.]

2. The following are children of/adopted by both [Partner 1] and [Partner 2] or are children of the family [this refers to stepchildren]

[insert children's names and ages]

1. ....DOB

2. ....DOB

3. ....DOB

4. ....DOB

5. ....DOB

6. ....DOB

3. Differences have arisen between [Partner 1] and [Partner 2] which make it difficult for them to live together as a couple. They have therefore agreed to live separately and apart.

Operative provisions

1. [Partner 1] and [Partner 2] agree that each will:

1.1 live apart as if unmarried.

1.2 be responsible for his/her own financial affairs and for the outgoings of his/her own home.

1.3 waive all rights to each other's pensions.

1.4 waive all rights to each other's assets under the Inheritance (Provision for Family and Dependants) Act 1975.

Legal lore

The Inheritance (Provision for Family and Dependants) Act 1975 states that if you die without making reasonable financial provision for your family and dependants, they can make a claim on your estate. And 'dependants' include your ex-husband or wife, unless they have remarried or a court order has excluded their rights under the Act. *This is why it is vital to get a court to ratify any financial settlement.*

1.5 Neither will make a claim on the other's property or claim a lump sum when the clauses in this agreement have been complied with.

1.6 The distribution of the contents of the former family home has already been agreed, and each will collect their share upon completion of all the transactions set out in this agreement.

1.7 In the event of both parties agreeing to a divorce, the court will be invited to make a consent order in the terms of this agreement so far as property and finance are concerned.

1.8 Each party will pay his/her own legal costs, if any.

[The clause below prevents you from running up bills in each other's names and makes each of you liable only for your own expenses.]

2. [Partner 1] agrees:

2.1 That he/she will not enter into any credit arrangements in ....'s name

2.2 That subject to .... making the payments referred to in clause 3, s/he she will maintain him/herself, and will indemnify .... from all other liabilities incurred In respect of him/herself.

[The clause below applies only where there is a family limited company. In practice, if this applies to you, you will certainly need to seek professional advice. If it does not apply to you, delete this clause and renumber the other clauses accordingly.]

2.3 That he/she will give up all interest in .... Limited, transfer his/her shares to .... and produce a letter resigning as director and company secretary confirming that he/she has no claim against the company for loss of office or otherwise and that he/she is not liable for any future company debt.

[Obviously, the clause below, which allows one partner to take on responsibility for the mortgage of the family home, would not apply if you lived in rented property. If it does not concern you, delete and renumber. If it does apply to you, remember to inform the building society.]

2.4 That subject to the consent of the building society he/she will take over sole responsibility for the mortgage on the

former family home at ....

.... [address]

and procure the release of .... from all liability for this.

[The clause below applies to cars on hire purchase. If it does not apply to you, delete and renumber.]

2.5 That upon .... discharging the outstanding finance

thereon, and upon ....

indemnifying .... in

respect thereof, ... will

indemnify .... from all further liabilities incurred in respect of the car registration number

....

[The clause below refers to property transfer and insurance policies. If this applies to you, you MUST seek legal advice. Apart from anything else, have you got your sums right?]

3. Partner 2 agrees:

3.1 That in return for the sum of £ .... pounds in cash [and the benefit of .... life endowment policies Nos

....

and ....] he/she

will transfer to ....all his/her legal and beneficial interest in the former matrimonial home at

....

[The clauses below provide for maintenance for both partner and children, including help with occasional needs such as school trips. They allow the level of maintenance to be reviewed without affecting the rest of the agreement.]

3.2 That until the first of the events referred to in clause 5 below, he/she will pay

£....................... per calendar month in respect of maintenance for

....

and ...., the first payment to become due on the signing and completion of this Agreement.

3.2.1 The above figure is to be reviewed from time to time in the light of the prevailing financial climate and the children's changing needs.

3.2.2 will in addition to the £...................... per calendar month pay

.... on request such sums as may from time to time be required for the children's school trips while they are of primary school age.

When the children attend secondary

school ....

and .... will each bear one half of the cost of such trips.

[The clause below deals with the family car; A hands it over to B without charge. Remember to inform

- the DVLC
- the car insurers.]

3.2.3 That he/she will for a nil consideration give up all interest in the car registration number ....

[The clause below allows the partner leaving the former family home to use that address for their mail until they are settled somewhere else.]

4. .... may if he/she wishes use the former family home at

....

as an accommodation address for his/her mail until such time as he/she purchases [or rents] a permanent home, ... to provide .... with stamped addressed envelopes for the purpose if mail is to be forwarded.

5. This Agreement ends automatically if:

5.1 .... dies,

5.2 .... dies,

5.3 .... and

.... resume living together,

5.4 any court order is made to cancel or vary the payments agreed above,

5.5 both ....

and ....

agree in writing to terminate or to vary this agreement.

IN WITNESS OF WHICH both parties have signed below

SIGNED BY

....

in the presence of

....

SIGNED BY

....

in the presence of

[The witness does not need to know what is in the document. Witnesses witness the *signing*, not the document.]

....

You and your solicitor

If you do decide to instruct a solicitor – and you will need to do so unless you are homeless, penniless and childless, you need one who is right for you. You could be spending quite a lot of money, so you should treat this matter like any other major purchase and do your homework.

People often have unrealistic expectations about their solicitors. Here are some of the things your solicitor should *not* be

- A counsellor.

  You are there for hardheaded practical advice, not therapy! All good solicitors have acquired some counselling skills along the way, but that is not what you are there for. And at £100 or more an hour this is a very expensive shoulder to cry on.

- A champion to fight for you, right or wrong.

  A good solicitor should give you sensible, balanced advice, not tell you what you would like to hear. If you are wrong, they should tell you.

- A friend.

  Do not confuse a friendly, sympathetic manner with friendship. There needs to be professional detachment for the good of both of you. Keeping things on a professional level will also save you money. Save your intimate chats for your personal friends, who are not charging by the hour!

Shopping around

Try

- The Solicitors' Family Law Association (see *Useful Contacts* on page 218). Ask it for details of family solicitors near you.
- The Law Society (see *Useful Contacts* on page 218) keeps regional directories of solicitors.
- Word of mouth: ask your friends.

The solicitor who did a superb job of conveyancing for your brother-in-law may not be your best choice for family law. Solicitors, like doctors, have their specialties.

- Surf the Internet. Try typing in 'family lawyer', 'divorce' and 'family mediation' and remember to press the button to limit your search to the UK! You could try adding your locality (eg, East Anglia) to limit it still further.

- *Yellow Pages*. Flip through the directory under Solicitors or access >www.yell.co.uk<

Check them out

In any case, you need to check the firm out for yourself. Here are some points to look for. Even if you expect to be publicly funded you are entitled to a good service for the LSC's money.

All solicitors must follow a client care code and you should, when you instruct one, receive a *client care letter* (see *Buzzwords*). A typical client care letter is shown on page 151. If you do not receive one similar to this, there is a strong indication that you should be looking elsewhere. Meanwhile,

- How efficiently did the reception desk handle your first contact?

If they seem at all untogether or unforthcoming, look elsewhere.

- How approachable is the solicitor or legal executive (see below) allocated to your case?

Good family solicitors are sympathetic and supportive, while maintaining a reassuring professional detachment. If you can't talk freely to the person allocated to your case you are going to find the proceedings very stressful.

- What are the offices like?

Scruffy, untidy, unattractive offices suggest a general lack of care and respect for both staff and clients. The offices of good family lawyers are usually family-friendly. There is likely to be a toy box for children – and a supply of tissues for you if you burst into tears while telling your tale of woe. We know of one solicitor who made such a hit with a small girl that, long after the family's problems had been sorted out, the child stopped at the office door and demanded to 'go in and play'.

A swift boast here – the firm of solicitors with which the authors of this book are associated was one of the first to be commended by the Law Society for its client-friendliness, and was featured in the national press and on radio. Pot plants, coffee, up-to-date magazines, a toy box and a welcoming atmosphere are not incompatible with legal excellence.

Need it always be a solicitor?

Many law firms employ matrimonial lawyers who are not qualified solicitors. Legal executives – often educated to degree level – are likely to be every bit as knowledgeable and efficient as solicitors in their chosen corner of the field, and their hourly charging rates may be lower.

Your first interview

Different solicitors have different techniques, but you should come armed with as much potentially useful information as possible. All this information will be required at some time during the proceedings. For example, the marriage certificate and all the details about the children will be required for any divorce petition:

- marriage certificate
- any official correspondence, such as any from the Child Support Agency, from your partner's solicitors or from your mortgage lender

- dates of birth for you, your partner and any children
- contact details, including home and work telephone numbers and e-mail addresses (if you have them) for you and your partner
- job details for you and your partner
- your National Insurance number and that of your partner
- details of the children's schools
- dates and places of any previous marriages, both for you and your partner
- if you are already separated, the date you separated.

You are also going to be asked about your financial details. Prepare a summary, including details of

- your income
- your partner's income
- any welfare benefits
- the approximate value of the family home together with details of any mortgages, etc.

Copies of any financial documentation such as pay slips and bank statements are always helpful. You might also have a stab at completing the financial form on page 154; it is all useful information for your solicitor. Before you hand anything over to your solicitor, make copies for your own file.

Supplying all the required information, and presenting it in an organised way, will save your solicitor's time and your money.

Take a pen and notepad with you and take notes. If you are feeling stressed you may not take information on board, or be able to remember it later, unless you write it down.

Emergencies

So far, we have dealt mainly with couples who separate by agreement – either formal or informal. However miserable they may feel about the break-up, they have at least set some ground rules and mean to stick by them. Nobody has been blatantly unreasonable.

Some people, however, have separation thrust upon them. They need short term protection – from violence, the threat of violence, harassment, sexual abuse or homelessness. And they need it NOW.

Where to go for emergency help

To seek emergency help, you can try

- Police – some may not be keen on getting involved in 'domestics' but attitudes have improved a lot in recent years, and they *are* available 24 hours a day
- NSPCC – if children are in danger – has a free 24-hour national linkline on 0808 800 5000; and see its website: contact details are in *Useful Contacts* on page 218.
- Social Services – also if children are involved
- Women's Aid Federation – national helpline on 0845 702 3468 and see its website: contact details in *Useful Contacts* on page 218.
- Solicitor.

Make sure you ask for someone who does matrimonial work. Many solicitors that specialise in family law are members of the Solicitors' Family Law Association (see *Useful Contacts* on page 218), an association of solicitors who are 'committed to promoting a non-confrontational atmosphere in which family law matters are dealt with in a sensitive, constructive and cost-effective way'. Click on the SFLA websitc >http://www.sfla.co.uk< for details of SFLA solicitors near you.

- Local authority housing departments – for emergency accommodation if you are made homeless.

Don't take risks, especially if you have children at home. Don't try to handle it yourself. Call in the professionals. They've seen it all before and they know what to do.

Domestic violence

This is what the law calls violence in the home rather than outside it.

Legal lore

Domestic violence is loosely defined as violence against a person by another person with whom that person is, or has been, in a domestic relationship. In other words, Punch and Judy for the 21st century.

Domestic violence can include

- physical abuse, including slapping, pushing and physical assault of any kind
- sexual abuse
- psychological abuse
- threats of physical, sexual or psychological abuse
- intimidation
- harassment
- damage to property, if it makes someone fear for their safety.

Additionally, allowing a child to witness any of these things, or putting the child at risk of witnessing them, can amount to child abuse.

If you are in this kind of situation, you need immediate help from a solicitor to get an injunction (see *Buzzwords* on page 10) to protect you and your children. This is not a DIY matter. You need the professionals – and...

That means a solicitor

Make an appointment, stressing that it is a domestic violence matter.

Consider staying overnight with a friend or in a refuge (look for Women's Aid in your local telephone directory) if you cannot get an appointment that day;

but most solicitors treat genuine emergency work very seriously and will move heaven and earth to squeeze you in urgently.

If you think you may qualify for Legal Help (see *Legal Help and Public Funding*, on page 77), you must bring your National Insurance number and benefit books with you.

Your solicitor is likely to ask you the following questions:

- Has there ever been any violence between you and your partner?
- Has either of you ever hurt the other?
- Are you afraid of your partner?

Your solicitor is also likely to ask you:

- Has your partner ever become violent after drinking alcohol or taking drugs?
- Does your partner lose his/her temper?
- Do you ever lose your temper?
- Do you often argue, and how often do your arguments end in violence?

You can be frank; it is difficult to shock a family solicitor, who will unfortunately have heard stories like yours many times before. Occasionally there are lighter moments. We were preparing the paperwork to help a 'domestic violence' victim with slight bruising to her arms and shoulders (consistent with being gripped with great force) when she suddenly said, 'I blame myself – I should never have gone for him with the carving knife'.

What about the cost?

In a real emergency there is no realistic alternative to instructing a solicitor to go to court to get an injunction to protect you from your partner's violent behaviour. You will need to go to court with your papers in one hand and your legal adviser in the other. Hopefully by the end of the day you will have your injunction, often with police powers attached (which means the police can arrest your partner if they try it on again).

Often, in emergency situations, the judge will allow you to apply for an injunction to restrain a violent partner without requiring you to inform your partner. This is called an *ex parte* order (see *Buzzwords* on page 9), and to make it legally binding the injunction has to be served on – ie handed to – your partner. Your solicitor will arrange this for you.

In certain circumstances, where it is reasonable for you not to let your partner know where you are staying, or if you are making the application on behalf of a child, you do not need to put your address on the application form. Instead, you give your address to the court on a special form which they supply.

Please read the section below. It applies equally to non-urgent matters, such as financial settlements and disputes over children: *do not assume that you cannot instruct a solicitor because of lack of money.*

Legal Help and Public Funding

This scheme is not only for emergencies, although you might first come across it in an emergency situation. It is available to anyone who needs legal advice and/or assistance and is too poor to pay for it.

A first aid dressing

Legal lore

What people need in an emergency is first aid. Many solicitors offer needy clients first aid free of charge in the form of Legal Help. This used to be called the Green Form Scheme because the form that solicitors and their clients signed was green. Today the form is no longer green, but it serves the same purpose. The form tells the Legal Services Commission (see *Buzzwords*) who you are and what your solicitor did for you. Afterwards your solicitors can claim their fee from public money.

Since April 2001 Legal Help has been *automatically* available only to people who receive

- Income Support *or*
- Income Based Job Seeker's Allowance.

You may, however, also be eligible *if* you receive

- Working Families' Tax Credit *or*
- Disabled Person's Tax Credit,

and get the maximum allowance. In some cases, if you get slightly less than the maximum, you may still qualify for Legal Help. Your solicitor will be able to advise.

If you are in employment but your income is low, you may be entitled to Legal Help if your income is within certain limits. For example, if (at the time of writing) you have no children or other dependants and your net pay is less than £87, then you will be entitled to Legal Help provided you have less than £1,000 in capital.

People with children can have slightly more capital and more disposable income per week and still qualify for Legal Help.

These rates were correct as of April 2001, but they tend to change every year, usually in April. Your solicitor will have the latest figures.

Good news!

A client who is separated from his or her partner is considered as a single person. So, even if your partner is a millionaire, if you have little money of your own you may well qualify for Legal Help.

This is a very simplified view of the Legal Help system. Your solicitor will soon tell you whether you qualify for Legal Help. If you do, they can initially do up to two hours' work for you free of charge, three hours in the case of advice involving preparing and issuing a divorce petition. For anything more, they may be able to extend the time they can spend on your case, but it is more likely that they will need to apply for Public Funding (see below) for you, particularly if they need to represent you in court, such as for an emergency domestic violence injunction, or what a client of ours called, memorably, 'one of them violent seductions'.

Public Funding (formerly called Legal Aid)

If Legal Help is a first aid dressing, Public Funding is full medical care: hospital, X-rays, the lot. It is different from Legal Help in that there is a scale of contributions depending on your means.

If you qualify for Legal Help, you will not have to pay anything at all for Public Funding, provided your financial situation remains the same throughout the proceedings. Otherwise your contribution to your Public Funding will be calculated according to your financial situation.

There is plenty of paperwork. Your solicitor will have to fill in at least two many-paged forms – one for the legal merits of your case, another for your finances – to apply for Public Funding on your behalf. Your solicitor will if possible use the time available to them on your Legal Help form to finance the paperwork for Public Funding.

In a red-hot emergency, your solicitor will be able to fax an application for Public Funding then and there, and your paperwork will catch up later. In non-urgent cases your application will work its way through the system until, if the application is successful, you will be sent an offer, which (if you accept) will entitle you to full legal representation under your Certificate of Public Funding. The offer will tell you how much you have to pay each month and also what work will be covered by your certificate.

Legal Help is immediate – your solicitor will decide on the spot whether you qualify. Normally Legal Help will be enough to cover the cost of obtaining a simple, straightforward divorce. A Certificate of Public Funding may, and usually does, take your solicitor more time to obtain on your behalf. In certain very limited circumstances your solicitor can speed up the process (see above). This will, however, only be possible in an emergency, such as where you need protection from a violent partner, or if you have good reason to believe that your partner may try to take the children out of the country.

Your certificate may be limited to certain items, such as investigative work, or it may have a wider scope. In some cases it may cover everything that is necessary to finalise matters on your behalf. In other cases it will take you just so far along the road before your solicitor has to obtain confirmation from another solicitor or barrister that your case merits further work, and therefore public money, spending on it.

The Statutory Charge

We know an old solicitor who used to explain the Statutory Charge as follows:

> Supposing I, through my skill, agility and daring, obtain for you millions and billions of pounds, or save you from losing millions and billions of pounds, do you agree – out of the said millions and billions of pounds – to pay back to the Legal Services Commission the money they will have spent on your case?

She would ask this several times during the proceedings to make sure the client understood the implications and could never plead ignorance if the Statutory Charge kicked in.

A more bureaucratic way of explaining the Statutory Charge is this: Suppose that thanks to Public Funding you obtain assets or money, or recover some assets or money from your partner, you must then pay your legal fees back to the government out of those assets or that money. This is called the statutory charge. It will also apply to assets and money which your partner has claimed from you and which you have managed to hang on to. Your solicitor should remind you about this several times and also hand you a leaflet, but we will spell it out now:

Public Funding is like a loan from the Legal Services Commission; a loan that you don't need to repay unless you obtain – or preserve – assets (money, property, etc.). In that case you may have to pay back your loan, which will enable the Legal Services Commission (formerly the Legal Aid Board) to help someone else. You can pay it back in cash, or have a charge (like a mortgage) on your home.

Divorce

I want it to be final – how do I get a divorce?

You can forget high profile divorce cases and courtroom dramas. Actually getting a divorce is very low-key indeed. It is, broadly speaking, a matter of filling in the right forms and waiting for your file to work its way through the system. Our flowchart shows how it is done. You can begin the process of obtaining a divorce in any of the County Courts but we recommend you use your local court, which is usually the court nearest to you. The courts are open weekdays, but not bank holidays, between 10 a.m. and 4 p.m., but will usually field telephone enquiries between 9 a.m. and 5 p.m.

Will I have to go to court?

Not in an open-and-shut case. While you get on with your daily life, a judge sits down with a pile of files and works through them. The judge agrees your application, and a few weeks later you are a single man or woman again.

Is that all there is to it?

No! Money, property, pension rights and so on are problems that must be dealt with whether you are divorcing or only separating. But it is not the business of the judge who is actually processing your divorce papers to be concerned with your property or your money. That aspect is dealt with separately – the buzzword is Ancillary Relief. At the divorce stage the judge just has to be satisfied that

- your marriage is over
- you have got the paperwork right
- any children involved will be properly looked after.

If the judge is happy about all three, he or she will sign a Certificate of Entitlement to a Divorce, saying when your Decree Nisi will be pronounced. Certificate of Entitlement? Decree Nisi? Don't get bogged down in unfamiliar expressions. Turn to *Buzzwords* on page 5 and trust us.

A path through the maze

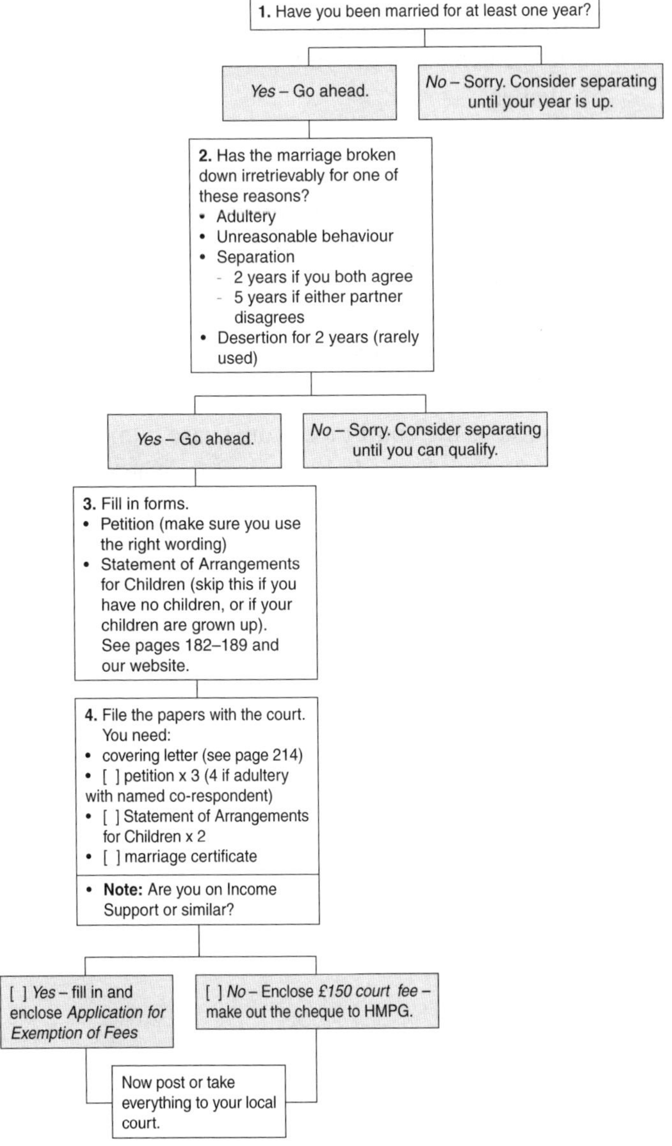

1. Have you been married for at least one year?
Yes – Go ahead.
No – Sorry. Consider separating until your year is up.
2. Has the marriage broken down irretrievably for one of these reasons?
• Adultery
• Unreasonable behaviour
• Separation
- 2 years if you both agree
- 5 years if either partner disagrees
• Desertion for 2 years (rarely used)
Yes – Go ahead.
No – Sorry. Consider separating until you can qualify.
3. Fill in forms.
• Petition (make sure you use the right wording)
• Statement of Arrangements for Children (skip this if you have no children, or if your children are grown up).
See pages 182–189 and our website.
4. File the papers with the court. You need:
• covering letter (see page 214)
• [ ] petition x 3 (4 if adultery with named co-respondent)
• [ ] Statement of Arrangements for Children x 2
• [ ] marriage certificate
• Note: Are you on Income Support or similar?
[ ] Yes – fill in and enclose Application for Exemption of Fees
[ ] No – Enclose £150 court fee – make out the cheque to HMPG.
Now post or take everything to your local court.

—You can often save time and tears if you discuss the Statement of Arrangements for Children with your partner before sending it to the court. Agree the arrangements and get your partner to sign the statement.

In unreasonable behaviour divorces, if your partner is at all co-operative, it is worth showing them the draft petition before sending it to the court, so that you can agree on the forms of words that are least objectionable to your partner. A little conciliation at this stage could save a good deal of hassle later.

As soon as the court gives you a case number, take a careful note of it and always quote it when you telephone or write to the court.

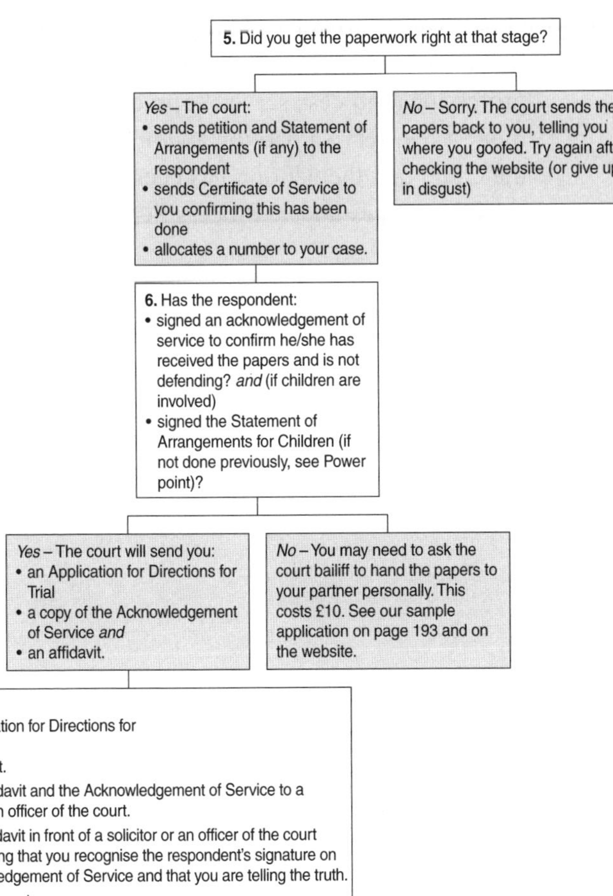

5. Did you get the paperwork right at that stage?

Yes – The court:
- sends petition and Statement of Arrangements (if any) to the respondent
- sends Certificate of Service to you confirming this has been done
- allocates a number to your case.

No – Sorry. The court sends the papers back to you, telling you where you goofed. Try again after checking the website (or give up in disgust)

6. Has the respondent:
- signed an acknowledgement of service to confirm he/she has received the papers and is not defending? *and* (if children are involved)
- signed the Statement of Arrangements for Children (if not done previously, see Power point)?

Yes – The court will send you:
- an Application for Directions for Trial
- a copy of the Acknowledgement of Service *and*
- an affidavit.

No – You may need to ask the court bailiff to hand the papers to your partner personally. This costs £10. See our sample application on page 193 and on the website.

7. Fill in
- the Application for Directions for Trial
- the affidavit.

Take the affidavit and the Acknowledgement of Service to a solicitor or an officer of the court.

Sign the affidavit in front of a solicitor or an officer of the court while swearing that you recognise the respondent's signature on the Acknowledgement of Service and that you are telling the truth.

Send to the court
- the covering letter (see page 216)
- the Application for Directions for Trial
- the affidavit with the Acknowledgement of Service.

Legal lore

The word *affidavit* comes from Latin *affidare* – to declare (on oath) – and means 'He, she or it has declared'. There. Now you can bore people at parties.

—Court bailiffs are a fine body of people, but may be less ingenious at finding the respondent than a professional process server. A process server will, for a modest fee, serve a petition and provide an affidavit to the effect that the petition has been duly served. Look in *Yellow Pages* under 'Process Servers'.

Dare we ask, however, why your partner is so inaccessible if you have talked this matter over beforehand?

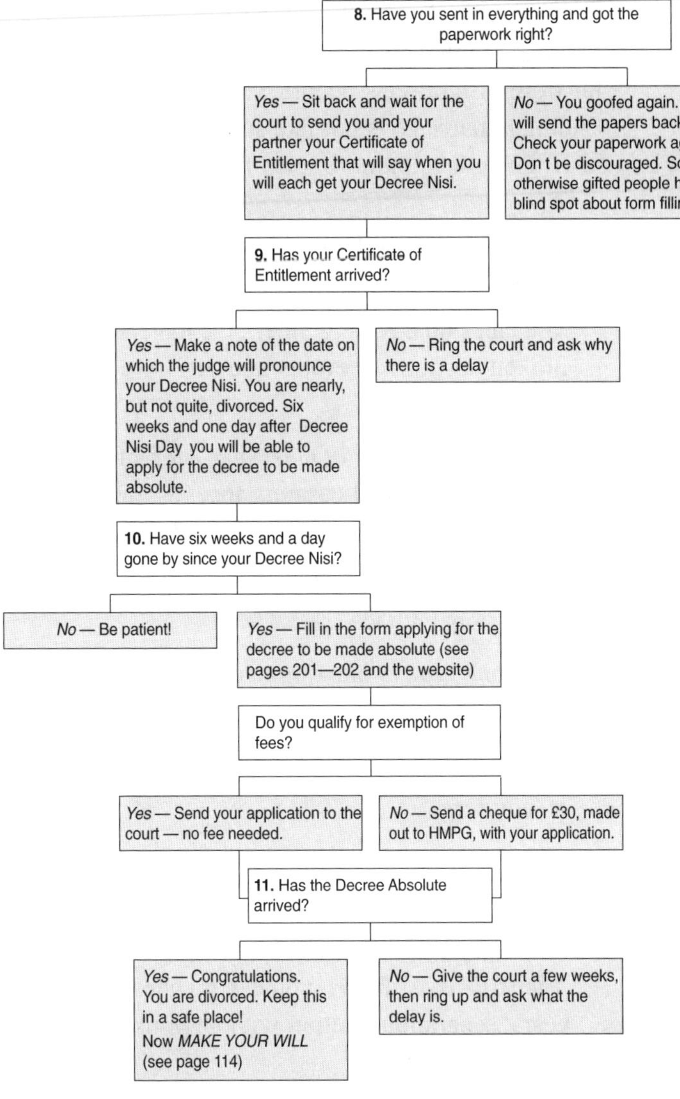
8. Have you sent in everything and got the paperwork right?
Yes — Sit back and wait for the court to send you and your partner your Certificate of Entitlement that will say when you will each get your Decree Nisi.
No — You goofed again. The court will send the papers back to you. Check your paperwork again. Don t be discouraged. Some otherwise gifted people have a blind spot about form filling.
9. Has your Certificate of Entitlement arrived?
Yes — Make a note of the date on which the judge will pronounce your Decree Nisi. You are nearly, but not quite, divorced. Six weeks and one day after Decree Nisi Day you will be able to apply for the decree to be made absolute.
No — Ring the court and ask why there is a delay
10. Have six weeks and a day gone by since your Decree Nisi?
No — Be patient!
Yes — Fill in the form applying for the decree to be made absolute (see pages 201—202 and the website)
Do you qualify for exemption of fees?
Yes — Send your application to the court — no fee needed.
No — Send a cheque for £30, made out to HMPG, with your application.
11. Has the Decree Absolute arrived?
Yes — Congratulations. You are divorced. Keep this in a safe place!
Now MAKE YOUR WILL (see page 114)
No — Give the court a few weeks, then ring up and ask what the delay is.

Some (we hope) helpful notes

You can see that, even with help and advice, divorce is far from instant! Few people would want it to be. Ending a marriage is not like selling a car or buying a hi-fi. There is a lot more form filling, for one thing ...

1. Have you served your time (ie been married at least a year)?

You can't do anything unless the marriage has broken down irretrievably and you have served your time.

Less than one year of marriage – forget it, unless – in very exceptional circumstances – you can apply to get the marriage annulled (see *Buzzwords*).

A nullity suit is not a DIY matter, however. Seek professional advice.

After one year of marriage you can apply for a divorce for

- unreasonable behaviour or
- adultery.

After two years apart, you can apply for a divorce on the grounds of two years' separation, with your partner's consent.

After five years apart, you can go ahead with a five years' separation petition without your partner's consent.

2. The Divorce Form

The different reasons for divorce are

- unreasonable behaviour
- adultery
- two years' separation
- five years' separation
- desertion.

If you have been deserted, use unreasonable behaviour instead, since deserting anyone is usually fairly unreasonable.

Spouses of persistent adulterers may prefer to cite unreasonable behaviour rather than try to list all the dates.

Until very recently there was a different divorce petition form for each category. Now there is just one. In theory this simplifies matters; but it does mean your form filling has to be spot on.

We print a sample form on pages 174–181 of this book, and you can download the forms and the accompanying Notes for Guidance from our website.

'Good form'

Here is a step by step guide to perfect paperwork and the procedure you must follow.

1. Find out the name and address of your local county court. We provide a list of county courts on the website. Telephone the nearest and check that fees

information mentioned in this book is up to date (it was on 1 September 2001).

You could also start your petition off at the Principal Registry at Somerset House in London.

2. Dig out your marriage certificate.

   If it has gone AWOL, don't panic! Replacement marriage certificates are obtainable from your local Registrar or the Registrar General in Southport. See *Useful Contacts* on page 218.

3. Fill in and sign your divorce petition (see our notes on each one on pages 95–106). Refer to the marriage certificate for the precise details of date and place of marriage.

4. Fill in and sign your Statement of Arrangements for Children – it is best if both parents sign this before filing with the court. See our notes on page 107.

5. Write a cheque for £150 payable to HMPG (Her Majesty's Paymaster General) or a form EX160 applying for exemption of fees – see *Important note* below.

Important note

People on Income Support or Family Credit qualify for exemption of their court fees. We have included, on page 190 and on the website, a Form EX160, to fill and send instead of the £150 cheque.

Free Legal Help?

People on Income Support, Family Credit or very low incomes also qualify for free legal advice and assistance under the Legal Help scheme. Consult a solicitor if you think you may qualify (see page 77 for fuller details).

6. Write a covering letter to the court (see the example on page 214).
7. Buy yourself a file and label it 'Divorce'.

   Now get yourself to a photocopier and take

   - three copies of the petition – (four copies if there is a named co-respondent)
   - two copies of the Statement of Arrangements for Children
   - one copy of your marriage certificate, because you will never see the original again after filing your petition
   - one copy of your covering letter.

Now send to the court

- the original petition and two copies (three copies if there is a co-respondent)
- the original Statement of Arrangements for Children plus one copy
- the original marriage certificate
- your covering letter
- your cheque.

Check everything carefully before sending it off, and keep one copy of everything in your file.

Form filling is not everyone's strong point; but court officials are very good at it. It is worth visiting the court and showing your paperwork to a friendly clerk to check you have got it right, rather than have it rejected.

Nitpicking accuracy

ALL the forms have to be completed in a very precise way. There are times when we suspect that court officials are carefully selected for their eagle eye and relentless pedantry. If you get anything wrong, the court will return your papers.

- If the marriage certificate says 'The Church of St Margaret' don't think that 'St Margaret's Church' will do. It won't.
- Likewise, you must take great care with names, dates and spellings. Your name, and your partner's name, must be exactly as in the marriage certificate (even if the registrar got it wrong on the marriage certificate!).

Don't say we didn't warn you.

Filling in the petition

Now for some heavy duty form filling.

Unreasonable Behaviour

Let's start with this one because it is the least straightforward. This is because you need to convince a judge that your partner has behaved unreasonably without bruising your partner's feelings so badly that he/she refuses to cooperate.

If your partner *does* refuse to play ball, you could find yourself with a contested divorce on your hands, which is emphatically not a DIY matter: seek legal advice.

Section 1

In the .... County Court

Put in the name of your nearest county court that handles divorces. You will find a complete list of Divorce County Courts on the website; check the address of your local one in the telephone directory.

Principal Registry

Cross this out unless you are petitioning in London and wish to use the High Court instead of your local County Court.

No. of Matter

Leave blank. The court will allocate a number to your case.

Section 1

On the .... day of .... the petitioner .... was lawfully married to .... (hereinafter called 'the respondent') at ....

You need to fill in

- the date of your marriage
- Your name (you are the petitioner)
- Your spouse's name (they are the respondent)
- the place of your marriage.

Copy this information from your marriage certificate. If either of you has had a change of name since then, you need to add either

- Name changed by deed poll, or
- Now known as.

Section 2

The Petitioner and the Respondent last lived together as husband and wife at ....

Insert the address where you last lived together as a couple. If you are still occupying the same house, this does not matter.

Section 3

The Petitioner is domiciled in England and Wales

If one or both of you normally live anywhere other than in England or Wales, seek legal advice. By the way, we have sometimes wondered how one can be 'domiciled in England **and** Wales' – a main residence and a weekend cottage perhaps?

and is by occupation a ....

Put in your job (or "Housewife" or "Retired" or whatever)

and resides at ....

Put in your current address.

and the Respondent is by occupation a ....

Put in your partner's job.

and resides at ....

Put in your partner's current address.

Section 4

There are no children of the family now living ***except***

If you have no children, cross out *except.*

If you do have children, fill in

- their full names (including surnames)
- their date of birth, or *Over 18* if this is the case
- if a child over 16 but under 18, whether they are
  - at school
  - at college
  - training for a trade, profession or vocation,
  - working full time.

Section 5

No other child, now living, has been born to the petitioner/respondent during the marriage so far as is known to the petitioner ***except***

If no other child has been born during the marriage, cross out *except*.

If you are the husband, cross out *petitioner* in *petitioner/respondent* but do **not** cross out *(so far as is known to the petitioner)*.

If you are the wife, cross out the word *respondent* in *petitioner/respondent* and cross out *(so far as is known to the petitioner)*.

If there is a child, such as by an extramarital relationship, living elsewhere, fill in

- the child's full name (including surname)
- their date of birth, or if over 18 if this is the case.

If there is any dispute about whether a child is a child of the family, please add a short paragraph saying so.

Section 6

There are or have been no other proceedings in any court in England and Wales or elsewhere with reference to the marriage (or to any child of the family) or between the petitioner and respondent with reference to any property of either or both of them ***except***

If there have not been any court proceedings in England and Wales concerning

- your marriage
- any child of the family
- any property belonging to you or your partner,

cross out *except*.

If there have been other proceedings (such as an abortive divorce petition in a different court), you need to leave except and then fill in:

- the name of the court in which the proceedings took place
- details of any court orders which were made and
- if the proceedings were about your marriage, whether you or your partner resumed living together as husband and wife after the order was made.

The might or might not affect your current proceedings. It is sensible to seek legal advice.

Section 7

There are or have been no proceedings in the Child Support Agency with reference to the maintenance of any child of the family ***except***

This one came in with the Child Support Act in 1993. If you have had no dealings with the CSA, cross out *except*.

If there have been any proceedings, give

- The date of any application to the CSA;
- Details of the assessment that was made.

Section 8

There are no proceedings continuing in any country outside England and Wales .... its validity or subsistence ***except***

This deals with proceedings abroad. If this means you, you need legal advice.

If there have been no proceedings in a court outside England and Wales which have affected the marriage, or might possibly affect it, cross out *except*.

If there are, or have been, proceedings, give:

- the name of the country and the court in which they are taking or have taken place
- details of the orders made or
- if no order has yet been made, the date of any future hearing.

Section 9

(This paragraph should be completed only if the petition is based on five years' separation).

You are going for Unreasonable Behaviour. Write 'Not applicable' below and go on to section 10.

Section 10

The said marriage has broken down irretrievably.

Don't write anything.

The Respondent has behaved in such a way that the Petitioner cannot reasonably be expected to live with the Respondent.

Don't write anything.

Section 11

They have left this blank. This is so that you can insert one of five paragraphs which they give in their Notes for Guidance. For an Unreasonable Behaviour petition you need their paragraph (b). Write 'The respondent has behaved in such a way that the petitioner cannot reasonably be expected to live with the respondent'.

Section 12

Here there is a space for the 'particulars' of your partner's unreasonable behaviour. The Petition should not contain a paperback book listing all your partner's bad habits, nor should it include a full history of your arguments and unpleasant incidents. However, you do need to ensure the particulars contain sufficient detail to satisfy the court that your partner has behaved unreasonably and has done so fairly recently. Bear in mind that what you regard as unreasonable in the extreme might not impress the judge at all.

Turn to our *Particulars* sheet on page 142 for suggestions. Always finish with 'Both parties are agreed that the marriage is at an end'. Then, even if the judge thinks your partner was not particularly unreasonable, he or she will heave a deep sigh and agree to a divorce.

Prayer

Not a pause for a swift *Nunc Dimittis*, but an appeal to the court to grant you

- a divorce
- your costs
- ancillary relief
  - for you
  - for the children.

Leave all this untouched, even if at this stage you do not want your partner to pay your costs or to pay maintenance, etc. A wise old family lawyer once said, 'They're easier to strike out than put in'. The matter in hand is your divorce; you will argue over the financial details later.

Signed

Do not forget to sign!

The names and addresses of the persons to be served with this petition are:

Fill in

- your partner's name and address
- your address (*address for service* just means the address the court is to send communications to)
- date
- the address of your local county court.

Now fill in the front sheet (which, confusingly, goes back to front at the back of the document. This is so that when the document is folded vertically all the details are immediately visible.

Adultery

This is a straightforward section to fill in. Everything is as above, until you get to section 11. But before you fill the form in, ask yourself:

- Have you and your partner lived together for more than six months after you found out about their adultery?

  If so, a straightforward adultery petition is no longer open to you. All is not lost, however; use Unreasonable Behaviour instead.

- Do you wish to name the co-respondent (your partner's lover)?

  There is no requirement for you to do so. In fact, in some situations you might not even know the Other Man/Woman's name! Section 11 of the form allows you the choice.

  If you feel strongly about it, however, you can certainly name the co-respondent, but be absolutely sure of your facts before you do so. And think hard before you do this if you want to avoid inflaming the situation. It might cost you dearly. If vengeance is more important to you than an amicable financial settlement, by all means name and shame. . . In that case, the divorce petition will be served on the Co-respondent as well as on the Respondent, which could contribute to another marriage breakdown.

  If there is any doubt about getting your partner to admit to adultery, or if you are at all hazy about dates and/or whodunit, opt for Unreasonable Behaviour instead!

  Now fill in the form exactly as in the Unreasonable Behaviour section above, except for section 11, where you write either:

- 'The respondent has committed adultery with a [man] [woman] and the petitioner finds it intolerable to live with the respondent' or
- 'The respondent has committed adultery with .... (*give the name*) (called the co-respondent) and the petitioner finds it intolerable to live with the respondent'.

Then go on exactly as before.

Two Years' Separation

You do not need to do anything creative here! Provided you put the names, addresses and, most importantly, the dates in the right places, you should be home and dry.

What's meant by 'separation'?

Preferably you should have been living under separate roofs throughout the two years. Otherwise, this is a difficult one to prove, though not impossible. See *Under One Roof* on page 32.

What about periods of reconciliation, during which you got back together? A brief get-together would not count, but if you get together for a month or more you may have to add that time to the two years. Separation involves a withdrawal from married life. Ideally you should live under separate roofs throughout the two years.

If you decide to have another attempt at married life together during your separation, but the attempt(s) fails, this will not prevent you from taking the previous period(s) of separation into account when totting up the two years separation, **provided** the period, or periods during which you got back together did not in total exceed six months. Brief periods of resumption of married life are disregarded by the Court, if they are less than, or total six months only. Longer periods might disqualify you altogether, or, depending upon the history of your relationship, may mean you have to wait for a longer time before you can apply for a divorce based upon two years separation with consent. You may be able to rely on part of the period you were separated, but because of a reconciliation, you may have effectively postponed the date you can apply for your divorce.

Take, as an example, Paul and Polly who separated in November 1998, but resumed cohabitation in January 1999 for eight months before separating again for good in September 1999. Although Paul and Polly initially separated in November 1998, they could not apply for a divorce, based on two years separation, in November 2000. They lived together for too long in 1999. Their period of separation only started to run again in September 1999. If they stay separated until September 2001, they will be able to rely on two years separation in order to obtain their divorce.

Molly and Mike on the other hand separated in August 2000, and lived together in October for two weeks before separating again. In November 2000 they had another try at living together, which fell apart before Xmas 2000. The total period they have lived together during their separation is less than six months and they can apply for their divorce, as soon as they have been separated for two years. Molly and Mike's brief time back together does not mean they have to start the period of two years separation all over again, as Paul and Polly had to in September 2000.

Now fill in the form exactly as before until you come to section 11. Here you write: 'The parties to the marriage have lived apart for a continuous period of at least two years immediately preceding the presentation of the petition and the respondent consents to a divorce being granted.'

Then go on exactly as before.

Five years' separation

Fill in exactly as before until you get to section 9.

Section 9

No agreement or arrangement has been made or is proposed to be made between the parties for the support of the petitioner/respondent (and any child of the family) ***except***

If no agreement or arrangement has been made, cross out *except.*

If an agreement or arrangement has been made between you

- about maintenance for either of you or for any child of the family
- about the family property,

give full details.

Section 11

You need to write 'The parties to the marriage have lived apart for a continuous period of at least five years immediately preceding the presentation of the petition'.

Then carry on as before.

Filling in the Statement of Arrangements for Children

What is a child?

For the purposes of the divorce petition, this refers to all of the petitioner's children, all of the respondent's children and any adopted by the petitioner and respondent, whatever the ages. You have to list them all in your petition together with their dates of birth. If they are over 18 you should say so.

For the purposes of the Statement of Arrangements, grown-up children do not count.

The Statement of Arrangements must include any child who was born to you and the respondent or who has been treated by you as one of the family who is either

- under 16 or
- between 16 and 18 and still at college or school full time.

This includes children born to either of you by previous relationships, and whom you have both adopted, but not foster children.

What sort of arrangements do you have to make? In the eyes of the court, the needs of the children come first. You too must put them first.

All this is set out on a court form, Form D8A. You will have to fill in

- the names and dates of birth of the children involved
- who they live with, and where, and whether this will be different after the divorce
- arrangements for their day-to-day care
- their health
- where they will go to school
- what financial support they will receive
- contact arrangements (visiting rights) between the children and the absent parent
- any special needs the children may have
- any care or court proceedings.

The court does not need to make an order about all of the things contained in the Statement of Arrangements for Children, provided the arrangements are in the children's best interests. In fact, the court would prefer it if you can deal with these matters amicably yourselves. If you have agreed the arrangements you can get your partner to sign the form before you send your various papers to the court. Otherwise the court will send a copy of Form D8A to your partner asking them to confirm whether or not they agree with the arrangements you are proposing.

If the court is not happy with the arrangements, it can make an order (known as 'exercising its powers under the Children Act 1989') changing the arrangements. Mostly, however, courts feel that it is better if the parents (and the children too, if they are old enough) can agree these things together. They are right. You and your partner really MUST cooperate on this matter if you want your divorce to go smoothly.

You may need to agree arrangements on other child-related topics, which may not appear in the Statement of Arrangements. Examples are

- arrangements for contact with grandparents and other relations
- school fees
- clubs and societies.

Let us suppose, however, that you and your partner are at loggerheads over the children. What will happen then? Well, the judge might decide to hold up your divorce proceedings until you are able to agree on satisfactory arrangements for the children. Then, if you are still at odds, he has several options, including

- asking you both for further information to enable him to make a decision
- asking you both to come and see him to discuss the problem. This will normally be 'in chambers' – in the judge's private room, with only you, your partner and the judge present
- referring you and your partner to a mediator, usually a Court Welfare Officer.

When the judge is satisfied that the children will be properly cared for, he will issue a certificate known as a D84B. This form makes it clear that the court has decided not to exercise its powers under the Children Act 1989. In open-and-shut cases this certificate is issued as a matter of course. If there have been disagreements the certificate shows the world that the disputes have been resolved and the court is no longer anxious about the children.

After the form filling – the next stages

See the flowchart. The court sends (serves) a copy of your petition and Statement of Arrangements for Children to (on) your partner. They now have eight days – starting from the day after the petition drops on their doormat – to respond. If you have filed an adultery petition and there is a co-respondent, he or she gets a copy of the petition too.

At the same time the court sends you a Notice of Issue of Petition which tells you when the petition was sent out. It will also give you your case number, which you must write on the front of your file in thick black felt tip pen – you will need it!

There is an example Notice of Issue of Petition on page 194. This gives a good idea of what to expect in this form.

Acknowledgement of Service

Your partner has to file an Acknowledgement of Service (see the example on page 195) and (if your partner has not signed it beforehand) the Statement of Arrangements for Children if children are involved – with the court within eight days, although the court will usually give some extra time, especially if the respondent lives abroad.

What if your partner does not return the papers? You can ask the court to instruct their bailiff, and we show you how to do this. See the sample covering letter on page 216. It may well, however, be more effective to instruct a process server. See the Power point on page 88.

It is, of course, sensible to make sure your partner will cooperate before starting proceedings.

Directions for Trial

Once your partner has returned the papers, the court will send you a photocopy of the Acknowledgement of Service together with an Application for Directions for Trial. There is an example of this on page 198.

Legal lore

Generals give orders. Judges give directions. An Application for Directions for Trial is not demanding a courtroom battle but merely a formal request for your divorce proceedings to go on to the next stage.

With the application is an affidavit, a questionnaire which you have to complete before swearing that everything is true. This questionnaire will vary depending on which kind of divorce you are applying for – that for separation is different from that for adultery, for example. The court will (one hopes) send you the correct form, although they have been known to goof, so do check for yourself.

Don't be hasty!

On the Acknowledgement of Service check the date when the respondent says he/she received the petition.

You cannot apply for Directions for Trial until nine days after that.

Check that the respondent has actually signed the Acknowledgement of Service – you will have to swear that this is their signature.

Don't sign the affidavit until the person witnessing it tells you.

Swearing an affidavit will cost about £7 if you swear it in front of a solicitor (if you are on Legal Help, keep the receipt and claim the money back through your solicitor). But if you swear before an officer of the court there is no charge.

Swearing is not a trivial matter. You will need to swear that the contents of your form are true. If you have any doubts, don't swear.

Now photocopy everything. Put your photocopies in your divorce file and then send to the court

- Application for Directions for Trial
- affidavit
- covering letter (see page 215).

Certificate of Entitlement

If you have got your paperwork right, you and your partner will each receive a rather unimpressive piece of paper headed Certificate of Entitlement to a Divorce. It will say that the judge agrees you are entitled to a divorce, and will give a date on which the Decree Nisi will be pronounced. Congratulations – you are nearly there!

If you receive anything other than a Certificate of Entitlement, it means you probably goofed in some way. Check your paperwork again; or consider ringing the court and asking where you went wrong.

Decree Nisi

Check the date, and mark in your diary the date six weeks and one day after the Decree Nisi. That is the date on which you can apply for the decree to be made absolute. Your partner will receive a Decree Nisi too.

Legal lore

Nisi is Latin for *unless*. And *unless* the couple decide not to go through with the divorce (which has been known to happen both in fiction and in real life), the next step will be the real thing – the Decree Absolute.

Decree Absolute

On DA Day, fill in the form on page 202 and send it to the court with a cheque for £30 payable to HMPG together with the covering letter on page 217. (Of course, if you are publicly funded you get this service free of charge).

You and your ex should each receive a Decree Absolute document. See the example on page 203. You can now hold a mild celebration. You did it all by yourself, you saved at least £500 in legal fees and hopefully you and your ex are still speaking.

Now keep your Decree Absolute certificate in a very safe place. And, if you have not already done so make your will.

Make your will!

Divorce affects any will you may have made before. It is always wise to make a will, and especially wise if you and your partner are at odds. If you delay in making your will and the unthinkable happens, your partner may get everything and someone you love may lose out. We remember a 29-year-old mother of three who died during divorce proceedings. We had sent her a draft will, but she had not yet signed it. Her drunken, violent husband got the lot.

You need our book on wills, *Write Your Own Will*, also in this series, to ensure that, if the unthinkable happens, your money and property will go to the right people.

Jointly owned property

Wills are especially important if you own a house jointly with your partner (see also *The family home* on page 123).

This is because, if the two of you own your home as joint tenants (which is usually the case), the other joint tenant will inherit your share of the property when you die. Suppose you died in the middle of divorcing the other joint tenant for adultery. Would you want your soon-to-be-ex, rather than your children, to inherit your share?

You can change this very easily by severing the joint tenancy so that you and your partner become tenants in common. This sounds difficult, but is in fact very easy; a sample form is on page 131 to enable you to do this. *Do remember to send it to your partner – it doesn't work unless you do this!*

A similar situation arises if the two of you have joint insurance policies. It is difficult to generalise; you would have to consult your individual insurer.

Dividing the spoils

Getting divorced is usually fairly simple. It is ancillary relief – the money and property side of divorce – that takes up the most time and causes the most trouble. You and your partner will need to draw up a list of what you own and what you owe.

Take advantage of all the free advice you can get. Most banks and building societies are helpful. Always tell them exactly what you are up to: why, for example, you are closing the joint account or making a new standing order. They may be able to suggest something you had not even thought of.

Consent orders

Even if you have handled your divorce proceedings yourself – and saved at least £500 in legal fees – you would be wise to instruct a solicitor to make sure the financial side of your divorce is legally sound as well as fair to both you and your partner.

Perhaps the best way of doing this is to get your solicitor to draft a consent order to be 'blessed' by the judge. The usual time to do this is between the Decree Nisi and the Decree Absolute. At the time of writing the court will not even look at a draft consent order before Decree Nisi stage.

A consent order is legally binding. It tidies up technical but potentially important matters such as excluding claims under the Inheritance Act and the Married Women's Property Act. The order closes doors that would otherwise be left wide open to potential claims – see below.

Legal lore

The Married Women's Property Act 1882 was a major milestone in women's rights. Before 1882 a wife's property belonged to her husband. If her rights under the Act are not specifically excluded, the wife will continue to have statutory rights against her ex husband.

Guidelines for ancillary relief

It is not the purpose of this book to cover ancillary relief (see *Buzzwords*) in any detail. We believe that if property and money are at stake you need to call in the professionals to advise on your individual case, rather than relying on general advice in a paperback book! It is, however, important for you to know the points a court would look at in making any financial settlement.

One of their key guidelines is a list of factors set out in Section 25 of the Matrimonial Causes Act 1973. It makes stodgy reading, but it is important and you should take it on board. The same guidelines would be used for Mr and Mrs Average and for the Duke and Duchess of York. The court must consider

- the income, earning capacity, property and other financial resources which each of the parties has or is likely to have in the foreseeable future, including any actual or potential increase in earning capacity, which either party may acquire or could take reasonable steps to acquire
- the financial needs, responsibilities and obligations which each spouse already has or is likely to have in the foreseeable future
- the standard of living enjoyed by the family before the marriage broke down
- the age of each partner and the length of the marriage
- any mental or physical disability of either partner
- the contributions which each spouse has made or is likely in the foreseeable future to make to the welfare of the family, including any contribution made by looking after the home or caring for the family
- in certain situations your conduct and/or the conduct of your partner
- the value to each partner of any benefit, which either spouse will lose the chance of acquiring, as a result of the divorce ending the marriage.

Many financial settlements are reached without going to court except to get a consent order 'blessed' by the judge; but the lawyers who brokered these amicable settlements would have taken into consideration all of these points. They would be aware, for example, that the court will not only consider any benefits under a pension scheme, which either spouse is likely to have, but would also take note of any benefits you, or your partner, might have otherwise enjoyed if you had not divorced.

The Matrimonial Causes Act headings provide the court with a starting point only and the court still has complete discretion to make such orders for ancillary relief as it thinks fit in all the circumstances.

Children

The court follows similar statutory guidelines when making decisions about financial provision for the child or children of the family.

These include

- the child's financial needs
- the financial resources of the child, including his/her income and/or earning capacity
- any physical or mental disability of the child
- the manner in which the child is being educated or trained and the way in which you both expected the child to be educated or trained
- the matters set out in the 'grown-up' guidelines, above.

Some financial considerations – ladies only

We told you – splitting up is simple if you are homeless, penniless or childless. Everyone else has all manner of financial loose ends to tie up. Here are a few.

National Insurance

Wives may have been paying the reduced rate NI contributions (the 'married woman's stamp'). If this applies to you, you MUST tell your employer as soon as your Decree Absolute comes through (or, in the case of a judicial separation, your Decree of Judicial Separation). You must then ask your employer to help you to inform the National Insurance office that you are no longer married. This, not surprisingly, requires you to fill in a special form, but your employer should have one in stock. You (or hopefully your employer) will then need to send the form to

Inland Revenue National Insurance Contributions Office,
Class 1,
Caseworker,
Long Benton,
Newcastle upon Tyne NE98 1ZZ.

If you do not tell the National Insurance Office about your change of status, you can be held personally responsible for any underpayment of NI which could affect your future entitlement to benefits and state pension.

If you are self-employed at the time of your Decree Absolute, you will become liable to pay Class 2 contributions from the date your decree came through. You must let the National Insurance Office know by completing a special form, which you can get from your nearest branch of the DSS or Inland Revenue.

Civil servants in the DSS and the Inland Revenue are ace form fillers. If form filling isn't your forte, go down to your nearest office and throw yourself on their mercy.

Benefits

If your Decree Absolute came through before you reached state pension age, you may still be able to get Incapacity Benefit (provided you're incapacitated of course!) and Job Seeker's Allowance if you have enough contributions and credits in your own right.

If you remarry before you reach State pension age, you cannot use your previous partner's contributions to help you to get a retirement pension. Your retirement pension will instead be based on your and your new husband's National Insurance contribution records.

If your marriage ended after you reached State pension age, then you may still be entitled to Incapacity Benefit and Job Seeker's Allowance, but these will be less than if you claimed Retirement Pension and when you reach 65 you should claim Retirement Pension instead. This is split into two parts, the basic pension, which is a flat rate, and the additional pension, which is earnings-related. You can use your ex-husband's contribution record to help you get a basic retirement pension if their contribution record is better than yours.

Both sexes – benefits

When you separate or divorce you may need to consider getting State benefits instead of any income you previously received from your partner. You may be entitled to Job Seeker's Allowance if you are able to work but are not working, or are working on average 16 hours or less per week. If you have children you may also be entitled to Child Benefit. People are only entitled to Income Support if they are

- over 16 years old
- on low income
- have savings under a certain amount (usually £8,000 but not always)
- not working *or*
- working less than 16 hours per week.

Anyone who is on a low income and paying rent can claim Housing Benefit, and they can claim Council Tax Benefit whether they are paying rent or not.

And of course if you have children and their other parent is living elsewhere you can claim child support from the CSA. It is commoner for mothers to claim, but fathers can too.

Pensions for people who are divorcing

If you divorce or get a Decree of Judicial Separation, any financial settlement or maintenance payments can be affected by the value of any pension you and your partner may have paid into. The court can order that most of this pension should be shared between you, even if it is in only one partner's name.

Note that if you separate but do not divorce, pensions cannot be shared in this way.

The family home

Rented homes

We're talking about protected/secure/assured tenancies here, such as for council or housing association property. If the tenancy agreement is in joint names, both partners will of course have rights of occupation/matrimonial home rights (see *Buzzwords*). Matrimonial home rights are basically a short-term right to stay in the family home until the long-term decisions are made. If the tenancy agreement is in the sole name of one partner (let's say Paul), his wife Polly will have matrimonial home rights until the fate of the family home has been decided, usually at the end of divorce proceedings.

Note that if Paul moves out and she intends to stay put, Polly *must* take steps to have the tenancy transferred into her name *before* the divorce is made absolute. This is because, by staying in the family home, she is keeping the tenancy alive under the 'deemed occupation' rules of the Matrimonial Homes Act 1983. Once Polly and Paul are divorced, these rules cease to apply. The tenancy will lose its protected/secure/ assured status, and there will be nothing for the court to transfer.

'Owned' homes

Let us suppose you and your partner own your own home, with or without a mortgage. It may be owned by both of you jointly, or it may be in the single name of yourself or your partner. If it is in joint names, your partner will have difficulty in selling or mortgaging it without your knowledge because your name would show up in the searches. If it is in one partner's sole name it's a different story...

In your partner's sole name

If the family home is owned by your partner in their sole name, you still have what some lawyers call rights of occupation and others call matrimonial home rights (see above). Your partner cannot exclude you, or legally evict you, from the family home, AND you can make sure he/she does not sell the house without your permission. We first mentioned this briefly in *Protecting the family home* on page 53. Now here is a more detailed explanation.

As long as you continue to live in the family home, with or without your partner, you have a legal right under the Matrimonial Homes Act 1983 to stay there until the court orders otherwise, or grants a Decree Absolute in your divorce. Until then, your partner cannot make you leave the matrimonial home, *provided* that

- you were living there together jointly, while you were married *and*
- you continued to live there without interruption, despite the breakdown of your marriage.

You will lose your rights if you move out of the family home. Even if you move out for a short period of time only, you risk losing your family home rights.

If you think you are, or may be, entitled to rights of occupation, but are not sure, because you spent some time away from the home, seek legal advice immediately. For example, a very short time – say a week – away from home will probably not invalidate your rights, especially if you have made it clear to your partner that you are taking a short break away, whether for a holiday, business purposes or to visit other members of your family, and that you are not moving out under any circumstance. At the opposite extreme, several months living with someone else with whom you are having a relationship will normally, but not always, mean you have lost your right of occupation.

You need the Land Registry

There are two methods of protecting your rights, depending on whether the legal title to your partner's property is *registered* or *unregistered*.

The Land Registry is the Domesday Book for the 21st century. Most homes will have titles (ie who owns them) registered at the Land Registry, because registration of title is now compulsory for the whole of England and Wales. However, there are some areas where registration used to be voluntary; and if your home is in one of these areas and you bought it some years ago, it is possible that the Land Registry has not yet got around to registering it.

Two people who might be able to tell you whether the property is registered are

- the solicitor who did the legal work when the property was bought
- the mortgage lender, if your home is mortaged.

If these investigations come to nothing, you can approach the Land Registry to find out whether the title is registered and if so, the title number given to the property. You do this by carrying out an Index Map search at HM Land Registry (see *Useful Contacts* on page 218).

Different Land Registry offices deal with different areas of the country and the way that their areas are split up is not always obvious. If you do not know which is the correct Land Registry for your area, telephone the one nearest to you and you will be told which Land Registry to use.

At the time of writing the Land Registry is changing its forms. Rather than publish something obsolete, we refer you to the Power point below...

Most Citizens' Advice Bureaux keep a stock of Land Registry forms and can help you fill them in.

You need to get a clear plan showing the location, situation and extent of the family home. It is possible to use a very large scale Ordnance Survey map, which you will probably find at your local library, sometimes on CD Rom. Get a copy and clearly mark the boundaries of the family home on your plan. Complete the application form (see Power point, above), attach the plan to it and send it to HM Land Registry. You should receive a result from the Land Registry in a few days.

If the property has an unregistered title, you need to protect your rights of occupation as the non-owning partner by registering a Class F Land Charge at HM Land Charges, whose address is also found in the address section at the back of this book. You must complete a form (currently K2, but see Power point above), showing the correct and full names of your partner as the person against whom the land charge is to be registered. At the time of writing there is no charge for this.

If the land is registered and you already know the title number, you do not need to make an Index Map search. If you believe the title is registered, but you do not know the title number you can either make an Index Map search or apply to HM Land Registry for Office Copy Entries of the title.

The Land Registry will send you the necessary form, which you complete and return to the Land Registry with the correct fee, currently £4. If you also obtain a copy of the filed plan relating to the property the fee is £8.

One advantage of getting office copy entries is that you can also check whether the property has been mortgaged by your partner without your knowledge. If it has, seek legal advice.

Once you know the correct title number, you can apply to HM Land Registry for registration of a Notice of Rights of Occupation against the title. Once again you can obtain the correct form from the Land Registry. You do not need to obtain your partner's title deeds in order to register either a Class F Land Charge or Notice of Rights of Occupation.

Joint ownership and the family home

All the above applies to a family home which is owned in your partner's sole name. Most couples own their homes jointly, either as *beneficial joint tenants* or as *tenants in common*. The main difference between the two is what happens to the property when one of the joint owners dies.

Beneficial joint tenants

If you own the property as 'beneficial joint tenants', the property will pass automatically to the survivor(s) in the case of death of one of the joint owners.

This arrangement is the usual one between married partners or cohabitees. The property will pass automatically to the survivor. So, if Bill and Beth are joint tenants, Bill will inherit if Beth dies first; and Beth will inherit if Bill dies first. This means that while Bill and Beth remain joint beneficial tenants neither can give away, either in their lifetime or in their will, any part of their share in the property. If either of them dies while still owning the property as joint beneficial tenants, the share of the partner who has died will automatically pass to the surviving owner.

Tenants in common

If you own the property as tenants in common, you will each own a distinct share (usually equal shares, but unequal shares are possible). Because your share is distinct, you can give it away either in your lifetime or in your will. When one tenant in common dies, their share does not automatically go to the survivor. So, if Bill and Beth are tenants in common, either of them can give away their share in their lifetime or leave it in their will.

If you are already beneficial joint tenants and wish to be tenants in common, giving your partner a simple form of notice will be sufficient to break the beneficial joint tenancy. A sample specimen of a notice, which will turn a joint beneficial tenancy into a tenancy in common is set out below.

Is the property registered?

For this to work, you will need to know whether your property has a title number. In other words has your property been registered at HM Land Registry, or is it still unregistered? You may be able to find out from

- the solicitor who acted for you when you bought your property
- your mortgage lender.

If you cannot find out this information do not simply decide not to serve the notice on your partner. Get the title number from the Land Registry (see page 219).

Now prepare the notice using the specimen sample below and give or send it to your partner.

– We've said it before and we'll say it again – if you decide to be tenants in common, you MUST make a will to dispose of your share to other members of your family. See our book on wills, *Write Your Own Will*, in this series.

Joint property – Notice to Disapply Rule of Survivorship

From: [your name and address] ______________________

To: [co-owner's name and address] ______________________

____

Property: [address and Land Registry number of ______________________

co-owned property]: ______________________

I give you notice that from today the rule of survivorship is not to apply to the above property, and that it is now owned between us as beneficial tenants in common in the following shares:

My share [ ]%

Your share [ ]%

Signed______________________

Dated ______________________

[on second copy only]

I acknowledge receipt of the original notice, of which this is a copy.

Signed______________________

Dated ______________________

- Do three copies. Keep one copy for yourself.
- Give your partner the original notice together with a copy and ask him/her to confirm he/she has received it by dating the copy and putting his/her signature in the box, which is on the second copy only.
- Your partner should then give you the second copy back for you to keep.
- Stash your copies safely away in the divorce file, which will probably be quite fat by now.

If you are the sole owner of the family home

– Stay put!

You do not need to take any further action at this stage, you should simply stay living in your property. But if your partner wishes to stay as well, note that they have matrimonial home rights until the divorce is finalised and you cannot, except in certain very limited cases, insist they move out. Even if your partner leaves the family home, they may still be able to obtain a court order giving them the right to re-enter and resume occupation of your property. If you want them to leave and they refuse, seek legal advice before doing anything more.

Managing stress

There are many books on stress on the market, but here are a few notes for starters.

If you press the thesaurus button on your computer and ask it for a synonym for 'stress', your machine will probably suggest 'pressure, strain, anxiety, constant worry, tension, nervous trauma, hassle'. Anybody who has experienced even the mildest marital disagreement has a first hand knowledge of stress in all its forms. This is not a book on stress management; but a book on marital breakdown without some reference to the accompanying stress would be like a book on cake making without any oven temperatures.

Which comes first, the breakdown or the stress? Well, stress is responsible for many marriage breakdowns, and any marriage breakdown is guaranteed to generate inordinate amounts of stress. Quite apart from our personal wretchedness and the misery our stress causes other people, stress affects decisions that should be rational and carefully considered.

When we are stressed, our decisions tend to be anything but rational and carefully considered. We are 'not operating on a full deck'; we are 'a few jewels short of a tiara'. We make dodgy decisions, or say unkind and ill-judged things, then wake up in the small hours weeping and sweating and wishing we hadn't. And so, if you are to save your marriage, or minimise the damage its breakdown does to you, you will need to manage stress.

Normal levels of stress are a necessary and important part of our lives. Without any stress, we would all be brain dead. Stress raises our state of awareness and arousal, improving our performance and making us more alert. Many writers work best under stress. Give them a tight deadline and they fizz with energy. Many matrimonial solicitors get a buzz out of emergency proceedings because they are time-critical and the happiness and even safety of a whole family may depend on *their* knowledge, skill, eloquence and perfect paperwork. Perhaps the best example of stress used creatively is on the trading floor of the Stock Exchange.

That sort of stress, in moderation – for we all need a chance to wind down or slob out from time to time – is creative and constructive. However, when the pressure intensifies to a point where the individual feels out of control, stress is harmful and destructive.

Stress can manifest itself in many ways. It can make you lose all confidence and self-esteem. It can affect your concentration and make you withdraw into daydreams. Stress can also bring feelings of tenseness, shortness of breath, difficulty in swallowing and even chest pains. Stress breeds mood swings, lack of enthusiasm, increased worrying, cynicism and irritability. It can make you 'hyper', rushing aimlessly about like a squirrel in a cage, or sluggish and listless. You may also become increasingly nervous and suffer from irrational fears and anxieties. None of these symptoms will help you to deal with the problems in your relationship.

Stress may cause behavioural problems, such as a withdrawal from family life or increasing dependency on 'comfort foods'. Scientists now know that chocolate in particular contains chemicals which enhance our natural 'feel good' hormones.

Bingeing on chocolate or chips is unlikely to harm anyone except you; but drugs and alcohol are a different matter. Different drugs have different effects, so nobody can generalise. Alcohol is more consistent. Heavy drinking, especially drinking on one's own, leads to irritability, selfishness, jealousy, uncontrolled anger and violent behaviour. Turn, if you can, to the biscuit barrel rather than the sherry or gin bottle.

Here are some stress-busting strategies that have worked for us, for our friends and for our clients. You can probably devise others that work for you.

- Write down what you are thinking and feeling and what is upsetting you. Then make the page into a paper dart and see how far it will fly.
- Talk to a friend about your problems. Even if your friend can offer nothing but sympathy, the intellectual exercise of expressing your problem in a way your friend can understand, can give you a lead to solving it.

- Recognise what is causing you stress. Face up to it and try to remove it from or reduce its impact in your life.
- Put the reason for your stress into context. Is it really as important as you first thought? Try asking yourself: 'In the terms of the history of the world, is this really so earth-shattering?' or 'Will I still be worrying about this in five years' time?'
- Try and look at situations and events in a positive rather than in a negative way. Sometimes the mere idea of doing this is so farcical (try seeing the positive side of your car breaking down on the dual carriageway, in the rush hour, in the rain, on your birthday and you'll see what we mean!) that you burst out laughing anyway. All the same, the optimist with a half-full bottle is happier than the pessimist with a half-empty bottle.
- Try and predict when a stressful event is likely to occur, so that you can prepare for it and deal with it more effectively. This is *not* the same as waiting in fear and dread for the worst to happen!
- Manage your time more efficiently – prioritise. People under stress often feel overwhelmed by the sheer logistics of getting through a quite normal day. Split the day's activities into small, manageable chunks. Then decide which chunks can wait. Unmade beds never killed anyone.
- This is probably a bad time to get a puppy, because all puppies trail stress behind them like Andrex. But make the most of any pets you may have. Walk the dog, longer and farther than usual, and enjoy the

uncritical affection. Stroke the cat (this is said to lower blood pressure and is in any case pleasurable for both of you). Consider giving a home to a kitten; they are less dependent than puppies and it is hard to feel tense with a kitten purring on your lap or chasing a leaf in the garden.

- Do something you might not normally do. Visit a stately home, gardens or museum. Take a one-day course in something new – aromatherapy, perhaps, or china painting. Hire a horse or a bike and go for a ride; or book a session on the police skidpan. 'Rosy's home stressbuster kit' – a long, luxurious bath, with a family of plastic ducks, bubbles in the form of bath foam *and* a glass of champagne, scented candles, Mozart on the hi-fi and *The Times* crossword – works for her. You could have a lot of fun finding out whether it worked for you.
- Take a large, squashy foam pillow and give it hell.
- Take control of your stress. Recognise it is there, and accept that you have to work within its restrictions.

Children

Your mantra here is: you and your partner, together or apart, will be parents for the rest of your lives. This fact must affect your relationship with their other parent. You want to be able to attend school functions together. Your children must feel able to invite both of you to family weddings, etc without worrying about possible 'scenes'. You may have stopped loving each other, but you and your ex must be courteous. After all, at work you may have colleagues that you heartily dislike, but you manage to be civil on a day to day basis. Is it so hard to do the same with someone you once loved to distraction?

You do not need to read many books about divorce to realise how harmful marriage break-up can be for children. You are bound to go through a bad patch. Reassure yourself that this is temporary. Talk to some couples who have been divorced several years if you don't believe us.

Breaking the news

Try to do this together. Work out beforehand what you want to say, and keep things positive. Children tend to blame themselves for their parents' marriage break-up, and lie awake wondering what they have done.

With younger children, stress that this is a problem for adults (we know one mother who said cheerfully, 'It's a grown-up thing, like a mortgage' and her child, who had tuned out many heated discussions of the family mortgage, understood instantly), and not in any way their fault.

Older children will want to be consulted. They may have clear ideas about whom they want to live with, and when they would like to see the absent parent. As they grow older, children develop quite busy social lives of their own and contact (see *Buzzwords*) arrangements should fit in with these.

Children might live with one parent for a while, then move to the other. We know of a boy who, after a couple of years with his mother, moved in with his father because the secondary school in his father's district had better facilities. This seems to us most sensible, and it is to both parents' credit that he felt able to do this.

Some practical points

You have probably thought about all these for yourself, but in case any of them slipped your mind:

- When handing over the children for contact, be nice. It doesn't cost anything to say excitedly, 'Here comes mummy/daddy to take you out!'.
- Encourage the children to exchange letters, e-mails and telephone calls with your partner between visits.
- When you talk to your children about your partner, resist the temptation to put the boot in. The children

love you both and can do without being asked to take sides.

- Go easy on the presents and cosseting. Apart from the fact that money is likely to be short, all the trips and treats in the world will not compensate for the break-up of a family. Kids are not stupid. We know of an 11-year-old girl who accepted all the blandishments of her previously violent mother with a shrug, saying 'I'll take anything she gives me, but she can't buy me'.
- Friends and local support groups can be a big help. We know of families who regularly hire a minibus for shared low-budget outings and other activities.
- Make your children's friends welcome in your home. It doesn't cost much to lay on squash and biscuits.
- Keep in touch with grandparents and other relations. It's unfair to deprive your children of half their relations because you no longer get on with your partner.
- Arrange child minding (a babysitting circle among neighbours is one low-budget solution) and get some social life for yourself. Being a one-parent family can be dreadfully claustrophobic and an evening class or dance session will do you good.

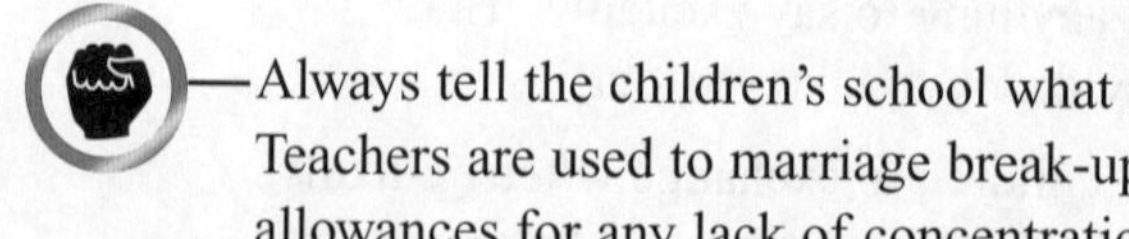

Always tell the children's school what is going on. Teachers are used to marriage break-up and will make allowances for any lack of concentration or behavioural lapses.

Court orders concerning children

If you and your partner can agree sensible arrangements for the children, you should never need to go to court at all, because there is no dispute. However, for the record, the courts can make four types of orders, known as Section 8 Orders because they come under Section 8 of the Children Act 1989. These are

- Contact order (in which, what the CSA call the absent parent, is applying for 'visiting rights').
- Residence order (to say which parent the child is to live with – the old word was *custody*).
- Specific issue order – an order of the court about a particular question that has arisen in relation to a child, and on which the parents disagree. This may concern religion, health, etc.
- Prohibited steps order – an order of the court to prevent something from happening without the court's consent, such as taking a child out of the country.

However, Children Act applications are emphatically not a DIY matter. Unless the matter is a dire emergency (in which case you should see a solicitor at once), disputes over children are best resolved amicably. We strongly urge you, before rushing into litigation, to contact an organisation such as NFM (see *Useful Contacts* on page 218) with a view to arriving at whatever solution is best for the children.

Unreasonable behaviour – particulars

***He spent her money and slugged her and killed her canary bird, and told it around that she had cold feet.* (O Henry)**

Divorce particulars are a bit like that: a blend of pathos and bathos. All these sample particulars are adapted from real-life petitions. We have omitted the really harrowing ones; you really would not want to know about the lady whose husband chained her up and forced her to watch while he pierced his own penis with a veterinary needle, or the husband who had to rescue his little daughter from a violent and sadistic mother. Here, however, is a real-life extract from a 1993 petition that we still find amusing – because the respondent is now the manager of a large DIY store.

The Respondent embarked on home improvement projects which always went wrong. He put nails through water pipes, built shelves that fell down and made a garden bench which collapsed under the Petitioner's mother during a family barbecue. The Respondent bought a new bath in a sale and put it in the bathroom but did not install it, with the result that for a year the entire family had to wash in the kitchen sink.

The particulars below are examples only. You would not need more than half a dozen. More would be overkill.

Financial mismanagement

Throughout the marriage the Respondent acted in an irresponsible way with regard to the parties' finances and would often provide no financial assistance towards the household expenses, leaving the Petitioner to take responsibility for this.

The Respondent was careless with money throughout the marriage and was unable to manage his finances, which was to the Petitioner's and the children's detriment. The Respondent was, however, able to finance a trip to______________________with another woman that cost in the region of £________.

The Respondent did not conduct his finances as though he were a married man; the Respondent was very secretive about his financial affairs and spent money freely, but not for the joint benefit of himself and the Petitioner.

Drunkenness

Over the two years prior to the parties' separation, the Respondent drank to excess. This resulted in the Respondent becoming abusive towards the Petitioner, sometimes in front of the child of the family.

The Respondent is an alcoholic, but refuses to acknowledge that he has a problem. The Respondent often vomits and urinates on the floor of the matrimonial home. The police, who have found him lying in the gutter, regularly bring him home. The Petitioner finds this unbearably humiliating.

As a result of the Respondent's drinking, there was a constant strained and tense atmosphere between the parties, which the children found disturbing and bewildering.

Throughout the marriage, the Respondent drank to excess resulting in him becoming physically and mentally abusive to the Petitioner.

Drunkenness and financial mismanagement

During the marriage, the Respondent drank cider or 'special brew' to excess, often five cans during an evening, to the extent that it affected his relationship with the Petitioner. The Respondent and Petitioner were both in receipt of state benefits, but the Respondent would put his enjoyment of drink first. As a result, at times there was not enough money to buy food.

Bad temper, violence and intimidation

The Respondent has an ungovernable temper and flies into a rage over relatively minor matters and disagreements.

On [date] the Respondent broke the Petitioner's nose, and on [date] he broke her collarbone. When, on [date], he started beating up the child of the marriage, the Petitioner left home, taking the child with her, and went to stay in a refuge.

At the end of April, the Respondent lost his temper and pushed the Petitioner to the ground. When she picked herself up, he pushed her down again. This caused grazing and bruising to the back of the Petitioner's hip.

Over the years there were many episodes of violence. On one occasion the Respondent threw the Petitioner and their children out of the house in their night-clothes. On another the Respondent grabbed the Petitioner by the hair. These are just two examples from many years of similar episodes.

The Respondent often intimidated the Petitioner. He recently threatened to smash the Petitioner's car, which he knows the Petitioner needs in order to get to work.

The Respondent has been violent towards the Petitioner. On [date], the Respondent, after placing a knife to his own stomach and threatening to kill himself, then grabbed hold of the Petitioner's throat with both hands and shouted repeatedly 'if I cannot have you nobody else is going to'.

Physical violence and sexual abuse

On [date], the Respondent became physically aggressive towards the Petitioner and had sexual intercourse with her, against her wishes.

Sexual problems

The two parties have not had any sexual relations with one another for almost two years because the Petitioner feels unable to bring herself to have intercourse with a man who has had so many adulterous relationships.

Since [date] the parties' sexual relationship has been non-existent. The Petitioner tried resolving matters with the Respondent, but he refused to discuss the matter.

The Respondent makes unreasonable sexual demands on the Petitioner and has on several occasions attempted to persuade her to take part in group sex, to the Petitioner's great distress and embarrassment.

Neglect of children and family life

During a trip to [place] in [date], the Respondent failed to acknowledge his/her son's birthday. The child did not receive a birthday card or present, or indeed a telephone call, from the Respondent.

During the marriage, the Respondent has spent

inadequate periods of time with his children, preferring to spend time enjoying his hobby of motor mechanics.

On at least three occasions during the marriage, the Respondent walked out on the Petitioner. During [date], the Respondent left the Petitioner for a period of three days and did not inform the Petitioner of his whereabouts. He was frantic with anxiety and the children were distressed and bewildered.

Until the Petitioner left the matrimonial home in despair, the Respondent worked late every evening and spent his weekends away from home, neglecting the Petitioner and refusing to discuss the possibility of spending more time together in an effort to save the marriage. He would never say where he was going to be, which worried the Petitioner because people would ring up and ask for the Respondent and she was unable to help: also he was unobtainable in an emergency.

The Respondent did not eat with his family or share in family life. In the mornings he took the leftovers from the previous night's dinner to his work and ate them there at lunchtime; in the evening he either ate something at work or brought home a takeaway late at night. This hurt and embarrassed the Petitioner, who would have liked the Respondent to share meals and family life with her and the children, on the basis that 'the family that eats together, stays together'.

Verbal abuse

The Respondent was often verbally abusive towards the Petitioner and would undermine her confidence and cause her to feel depressed and unhappy.

The Respondent would often shout at the Petitioner and threaten her. He would tell her to shut up otherwise he would get angry.

Dishonesty

Throughout the marriage, the Respondent would lie to the Petitioner causing her great anguish and distress.

Jealousy and possessiveness

While the Respondent would go out and socialise on his own with his friends, he would not permit the Petitioner to do the same.

While on holiday in Spain during September 2000, with the Petitioner's sister, the Respondent would not permit the Petitioner to go out with her sister.

The Respondent was obsessively jealous and refused to permit the Petitioner to have any friends of her own or any social life, interests or pursuits outside the matrimonial home.

Mild unreasonableness

Throughout the marriage the Respondent was selfish and inconsiderate towards the Petitioner and took little or no account of the Petitioner's wishes and feelings.

On or about 12 June 2001, the Respondent accused the Petitioner of taking him for granted and stated that she did not love the Petitioner any more.

The Respondent has repeatedly stated to the Petitioner that he wants his freedom.

Generally, throughout the marriage, the Respondent has failed to treat the Petitioner with the respect, care and affection to which she was entitled as his wife and as a woman.

The Respondent refused to allow the Petitioner the use of the family car to go to her evening classes.

The Respondent was a dirty and inefficient housekeeper, who frequently left piles of dirty laundry lying about.

The Respondent was threatening, domineering and patronising towards the Petitioner with the result that the Petitioner constantly felt 'smothered' by her during the marriage. The Respondent constantly told the Petitioner that she was ashamed of him.

During the five months prior to the date of this petition, the Respondent has increasingly picked arguments with the Petitioner about petty matters such as domestic chores not done and being unable to find various items. These arguments have become increasingly heated and upsetting for the Petitioner who is concerned that the yelling and shouting will upset the children of the family.

The parties' sexual relations ceased some three to four months prior to the date of this petition.

Sample documents and official forms

Sample Client Care Letter

A good solicitor will send you a client care letter, which should read roughly like this one.

Dear ......

1. We aim to provide you with a friendly, prompt and efficient service

2. We will treat your affairs with complete confidentiality.

3. We will use our best efforts to:

   i. return your telephone calls withint two hours.
   ii. answer your letters and faxes by return,
   iii. see you within one working day if you want an appointment,
   iv. see you immediately if your case is urgent.

4. If we have given you an estimate, we will:

   i. carry out our work for you at the estimated fee, subject to the conditions which the estimates states,
   ii. if the estimate is for a matter which, for any reason, is not completed we will charge you for the work already done, plus expenses incurred. Similarly, if you ask us to do further work outside the scope of the estimate, we will make an additional charge.

5. If we have not given you an estimate, we will charge you on a time basis at an hourly rate. This rate may vary in accordance with urgency, importance, value, expertise and responsibility. If relevant, we will set out below the hourly rate for the work we do for you.

6. If we hold money for you, we will place it in our general client account i.e. a separate bank deposit account we have for any money which belongs to you the client – not to us. In the case of large sums held over a long period, we will open an individual account for you. If you request, and subject to the Solicitors' Accounts Rules 1991, we will pay you the interest net of basic rate tax.

7. We are authorised to conduct investment business and we can offer financial advice either on a fee basis, that is by charging an hourly rate for our work, or on a commission basis, from the sale of financial products.

8. If you have any complaint about our service, please tell us. You should speak first to .... If you are still dissatisifed, you have the right to complain to the office for the Supervision of Solicitors, Victoria Court,
8 Dormer Place, Leamington Spa, Warwicks,
CV32 5AE, telephone 01926 820082.

The person dealing with your affair is:

If s/he is not available, you should speak to:

If applicable, the hourly rate we will charge you is £ plus VAT and expenses. In addition to this we will charge 10 pc of the hourly rate plus VAT for each telephone call, letter and fax.

Financial Statement

This is the financial statement which a mediator would ask you to fill in. The court would use a similar form to help with ancillary relief applications. We have suggested you use it to help you to work out your income and outgoings.

Sample financial statement

FINANCIAL STATEMENT

[Applicant][Respondent]

In the	
*[County Court] *[Principal Registry of the Family Division]	
Case No. *Always quote this*	

(delete as appropriate)

Between Applicant

Solicitor's Ref:

and

Respondent

Solicitor's Ref:

Please fill in this form fully and accurately. Where any box is not applicable write "N/A". You have a duty to the court to give a full, frank and clear disclosure of all your financial and other relevant circumstances.

A failure to give full and accurate disclosure may result in any order the court makes being set aside.

If you are found to have been deliberately untruthful, criminal proceedings for perjury may be taken against you.

You must attach documents to the form where they are specifically sought and you may attach other documents where it is necessary to explain or clarify any of the information that you give.

Essential documents, which **must** accompany this Statement, are detailed at questions 2.1, 2.2, 2.3, 2.5, 2.14, 2.18 and 2.20.

If there is not enough room on the form for any particular piece of information, you may continue on an attached sheet of paper.

This statement must be sworn before an Officer of the Court,
a Solicitor or a Commissioner for Oaths
before it is filed with the Court
or sent to the other party
(see page 20).

Form F Financial Statement 1

Part 1 General Information

1.1 Full Name

1.2 Date of Birth

Date	Month	Year

1.3 Date of Marriage

Date	Month	Year

1.4 Occupation

1.5 Date of the separation

Date	Month	Year	Tick here ☐ if not applicable

1.6 Date of the:

Petition			Decree Nisi/Decree of Judicial Separation			Decree Absolute		
Date	Month	Year	Date	Month	Year	Date	Month	Year

1.7 If you have remarried, or will remarry, state the date

Date	Month	Year

1.8 Do you live with another person? ☐ Yes ☐ No

1.9 Do you intend to live with someone within the next six months? ☐ Yes ☐ No

1.10 Details of any children of the family

Full names	Date of Birth			With whom does the child live?
	Date	Month	Year	

1.11 Give details of the state of health of yourself and the children

Yourself	Children

2

1.12 Give details of the present and proposed future educational arrangements for the children.

Present arrangements	Future arrangements

1.13 Give details of any Child Support Maintenance Assessments or Child Maintenance Orders made between the parties. If no assessment or agreement has been made, give an estimate of the liability of the non-residential parent under the Child Support Act 1991, in respect of the children of the family.

1.14 If this application is to vary an order, give details of the order that is to be varied and attach a copy of the order. Give the reasons for asking for the order to be varied.

1.15 Give details of any other court cases between you and your husband/wife, whether in relation to money, property, children or anything else.

Case No.	Court

1.16 Specify your present residence and the occupants of it and on what terms you occupy it (e.g. tenant, owner-occupier).

Address	Occupants	Terms of occupation

Part 2 Financial Details *Capital: Realisable Assets*

** If you have obtained a valuation within the last six months attach a copy. If not, give your own estimate of the property value. A copy of your most recent mortgage statement is also required.*

2.1 Give details of your interest in the matrimonial home.

Property name and address	Land Registry Title No.	Nature and extent of your interest	*Property value

Mortgagee's Name and address	Type of mortgage	Balance outstanding on any mortgage	Total current value of your beneficial interest
1st			
2nd			
Other:			
		NET value of your interest in the matrimonial home (A)	£

2.2 Give details of all other properties, land, and buildings in which you have an interest.

Property name(s) and address(es)	Land Registry Title No.	Nature and extent of your interest	*Property value
1.			
2.			
3.			

Mortgagee's Name(s) and address(es)	Type of mortgage	Balance outstanding on any mortgage	Total current value of your interest
1.			
2.			
3.			
		TOTAL value of the above (not including the matrimonial home)	(B1) £

4

2.3 Give details of all bank, building society, and National Savings accounts, in credit, which you hold or have an interest in. Include all PEPs, TESSAs and ISAs. For joint accounts, give your interest and the name of the account holder. If the account is overdrawn, include in Liabilities section at 2.12
You must attach your bank statements covering the last 12 months for each account listed

Name of bank or building society including Branch name	Type of account (e.g. current)	Account number	Name of other account holder *(if applicable)*	Balance at the date of this Statement	Total current value of your interest
1.					
2.					
3.					
4.					
5.					

TOTAL value of your interest in ALL accounts (B2) £

2.4 Give details of all stocks, gilts and other quoted securities which you hold or have an interest in.
Do not include dividend income as this will be dealt with separately later on.

Name	Type	Size	Current value	Total current value of your interest

TOTAL value of your interest in ALL holdings (B3) £

2.5 Give details of all life insurance policies which you hold or in which you have an interest, including those that do not have a surrender value, for each policy.

Policy details including name of company, policy type and number	If policy is charged, state in whose favour and amount of charge	Maturity date			Surrender Value	Total current value of your interest
		Date	Month	Year		

You must attach any surrender value quotations

TOTAL value of your interest in ALL policies (B4) £

5

2.6 Give details of all issues of National Savings Certificates which you hold or have an interest in.

Name of issue	Nominal amount	Current value	Total current value of your interest

TOTAL value of ALL your certificates (B5) £

2.7 Give details of all of National Savings Bonds (including Premium Bonds) and other bonds which you hold or have an interest in.

Type of Bond	Bond holder's number	Current value	Total current value of your interest

TOTAL value of ALL your bonds (B6) £

2.8 Give details of all monies which are OWED TO YOU. Include sums owed in director's or partnership accounts.

Brief description of debt	Balance outstanding	Total current value of your interest

TOTAL value of your interest in ALL debts owed to you (B7) £

6

2.9 Give details of all of cash savings held in excess of £300. You must state where it is held and the currency it is held in.

Where held	Amount	Currency	Total current value of your interest

TOTAL value of ALL your cash (B8) £

2.10 Give details of personal belongings individually worth more than £500.
Include cars (gross value), collections, pictures, jewellery, furniture, and household belongings (this list is not exhaustive).

Item	Sale value	Total estimated current value of your interest

TOTAL value of your interest in ALL personal belongings (B9) £

2.11 Give details of any other realisable assets not yet mentioned, for example, unit trusts, investment trusts, commodities, business expansion schemes and futures (this list is not exhaustive).
This is where you must mention any other realisable assets.

Type	Current value	Total current value of your interest

TOTAL value of your interest in ALL other realisable assets (B10) £

Now add together all the figures in the previous total boxes (B1 to B10) to give the TOTAL current value of ALL your interest in realisable assets.

(B) £

7

Part 2 Financial Details *Capital: Liabilities*

2.12 Give details of any liabilities you have. Exclude mortgages on property dealt with above. **Include** money owed on credit cards and store cards, bank loans, hire purchase agreements and any overdrawn bank or building society accounts.

Liability (i.e. total amount owed, current monthly payments and term of loan/debt)	Current amount	Total current value of your share of the liability

TOTAL value of ALL your liabilities (C1) £

Part 2 Financial Details *Capital: Capital Gains Tax*

2.13 If any Capital Gains Tax would be payable on the disposal now of any of your realisable assets, give your estimate of the tax.

Asset	Capital Gains Tax	Total current value of your liability

TOTAL value of ALL your Capital Gains Tax liabilities (C2) £

Now add together C1 + C2 to give:-
TOTAL net value of your liabilities **(C)** £

Now take the liabilities total from the realisable assets total (A+B-C), to give:-
TOTAL net value of your personal assets **(D)** £

8

Part 2 Financial Details *Capital: Business Assets*

2.14 Give details of all your business interests. *You must attach a copy of the last 2 years accounts and any other document on which you base your valuation.*

Name and nature of your business	Your ESTIMATE of the current value of your interest	Your ESTIMATE of any possible Capital Gains Tax payable on disposal	Basis of valuation *(No formal valuation is required at this time)*	What is the extent of your interest?	Total net current value of your interest

TOTAL current value of your interest in business assets (E) £

2.15 List any directorships you hold or held in the last 12 months

9

Part 2 Financial Details *Capital: Pensions (including SERPS but excluding Basic State Pensions)*

2.16 Give details of your pension interests.

If you have been provided with a valuation of your pension rights by the trustees or managers of the pension scheme you must attach it. Where the information is not available, give the estimated date when it will be available and attach the letter to the pension company or administrators from whom the information was sought. If you have more than one pension plan or scheme, you must provide the information in respect of each one, continuing, if necessary, on a separate piece of paper. If you have made Additional Voluntary Contributions or any Free Standing Additional Voluntary Contributions to any plan or scheme, you must give the information separately if the benefits referable to such contributions are separately recorded or paid. If you have more than one pension scheme you should reproduce the information for each scheme. Please include any SERPS.

Information about the Scheme(s)

Name and address of scheme, plan or policy	
Your National Insurance number	
Number of scheme, plan or policy	
Type of scheme, plan or policy *(e.g. final salary, money purchase or other)*	

CETV - Cash Equivalent Transfer Value

CETV Value	
The lump sum payable on death in service before retirement	
The lump sum payable on death in deferment before retirement	
The lump sum payable on death after retirement	

Retirement Benefits

Earliest date when benefit can be paid	
The estimated lump sum and monthly pension payable on retirement, assuming you take the maximum lump sum	
The estimated monthly pension without taking any lump sum	

Spouse's Benefit

On death in service	
On death in deferment	
On death in retirement	

Dependant's Benefit

On death in service	
On death in deferment	
On death in retirement	

TOTAL value of your pension assets (F) £

10

Part 2 Financial Details *Capital: Other Assets*

2.17 Give details of any other assets not listed above.
Include the following: (this list is not exhaustive)

- **Unrealisable assets.**
- **Share option scheme,** stating the estimated net sale proceeds of the shares if the options were capable of exercise now, and whether Capital Gains Tax or Income Tax would be payable.
- **Trust interests** (including interests under a discretionary trust), stating your estimate of the value of the interest and when it is likely to become realisable. If you say it will never be realisable, or has no value, give your reasons.
- Specify also any asset that is likely to be received in the foreseeable future, any assets held on your behalf by a third party and any assets not mentioned elsewhere in this form held outside England and Wales.

Type of Asset	Value	Total net value of your interest

TOTAL value of your other assets (G) £

TOTAL value of your net assets (excluding pensions) (D+E+G) (H) £

TOTAL value of your net assets (including pensions) (H+F) (I) £

11

Part 2 Financial Details *Income*

You must attach your last three payslips and your P60 for the most recently completed financial year

2.18 Earned Income: Give details of your gross and net income in the last financial year, and in the current financial year.

Nature of income (e.g. salary, bonus)	Last financial year		Current financial year *(estimated for the whole year)*	
	Gross	Net	Gross	Net

2.19 Additional Income: benefits etc. Give details and the value of all benefits in kind, perks, or other remuneration not disclosed elsewhere, received in the last financial year and current financial year.

Nature of income	Last financial year	Current financial year *(estimated for the whole year)*

12

Income continued

2.20 Self-employed or partnership income: Give details of annual net profit or loss for the last two accounting years, your share of this figure and tax payable to date of the last accounts and the estimate of income since that date. State the date on which your accounting year begins. Year 2 should be the most recent year, Year 1 the previous year. Please state the "from" and "to" dates for the years concerned.

Nature of income and date your accounting year begins	Details of the last two accounting periods					
	Net profit/loss		Your share of profit/loss		Tax payable by you	
	Year 1	Year 2	Year 1	Year 2	Year 1	Year 2
Net income SINCE date of last accounts and estimate for the whole year	Net Income	Estimate	*You must attach the accounts for the last two completed accounting years*			

2.21 Investment income (e.g. dividends, interest) Give details of net income received in the last financial year, and in the current financial year and state whether it was paid gross or net of income tax. You are not required to calculate any tax payable that may arise.

Nature of income and the asset from which it derived	Paid gross or net *(delete that which is not applicable)*	Last financial year	Current financial year
	Gross/Net		

2.22 State benefits (including state pension) Give details of all state benefits received in the last 52 weeks

Nature of income	Total income received in the last 52 weeks

13

2.23 Any other income Give details of any other income received in the last 52 weeks

Nature of income	Total income for the last 52 weeks

Part 2 Financial Details *Summaries*

2.24 Summary of your income

Your estimate of your current annual net income from all sources (2.18 - 2.23)	Your estimate of your net income from all sources for the next 52 weeks
£	£ (J)

2.25 Summary of financial information

	Reference of the section on this statement	Value
Net value of your interest in the matrimonial home	A	
Total current value of all your interest in the other realisable assets	B	
Total net value of your liabilities	C	
Total net value of your personal assets	D	
Total current value of your interest in business assets	E	
Total current value of your pension or transfer values	F	
Total value of your other assets	G	
Total value of your net assets *(excluding pension)*	H	
Total value of your net assets *(including pension)*	I	
Total estimated net income for the next 52 weeks	J	

14

Part 3 Requirements *Income Needs*

3.1 Give the reasonable future income needs of yourself (e.g. housing, car etc) and of any children living with you, or provided for by you. This may be expressed as annual, monthly or weekly figures (state which), but you should not use a combination of any of these periods.

Item	*Income needs of yourself*	Amount
	sub-total	

Item	*Income needs of child(ren) living with you, or provided for by you*	Amount
	sub-total	
	TOTAL income needs	£

15

Part 3 Requirements *Capital Needs*

3.2 Give the reasonable future capital needs of yourself and of any children living with you, or provided for by you.

Item	*Capital needs of yourself*	Cost
	sub-total	

Item	*Capital needs of child(ren) living with you, or provided for by you.*	Cost
	sub-total	
	TOTAL capital needs	£

16

Part 4 Other Information

4.1 State whether there has been any significant change in your net assets during the last 12 months, including any assets held outside England and Wales (e.g. closure of any bank or building society accounts).

4.2 Give brief details of the standard of living enjoyed by you and your spouse during the marriage.

4.3 Are there any particular contributions to the family property and assets or outgoings, or to family life, that have been made by you, your partner or anyone else that you think should be taken into account? If so, give a brief description of the contribution, the amount, when it was made, and by whom.

4.4 Bad behaviour or conduct by the other party will only be taken into account in very exceptional circumstances when deciding how the assets should be divided after divorce. If you feel it should be taken into account in your case identify the nature of the behaviour or conduct.

17

Part 4 Other Information *continued*

4.5 Give details of any other circumstances which you consider could significantly affect the extent of the financial provision to be made by or for you or for any child of the family e.g. earning capacity, disability, inheritance prospects or redundancy, remarriage and cohabitation plans, any contingent liabilities.
(This list is not exhaustive).

4.6 If you have remarried (or intend to) or are living with another person (or intend to), give brief details, so far as they are known to you, of his or her income and assets.

Annual Income		Assets	
Nature of Income	Value (state whether gross or net, if known)	Item	Value (if known)
Total:		Total:	

18

Part 5 Order Sought

5.1 **If you are able to at this stage, specify what kind of orders you are asking the court to make, and state whether at this stage you see the case being appropriate for a "clean break".** (A "clean break" means a settlement or order which provides, amongst other things, that neither you nor your spouse will have any further claim against the income or capital of the other party. A clean break does not terminate the responsibility of a parent to a child).

5.2 ****If you are seeking a transfer or settlement of any property or other asset, you must identify the asset in question.**

5.3 ****If you are seeking a variation of a pre-nuptial or post-nuptial settlement, you must identify the settlement, by whom it was made, its trustees and beneficiaries, and state why you allege it is a nuptial settlement.**

** **Important Note:** Where 5.2, 5.3 (above) or 5.4 (overleaf) apply, you should seek legal advice before completing the sections.

Part 5 Order Sought *continued*

5.4 **If you are seeking an avoidance of disposition order, you must identify the property to which the disposition relates and the person or body in whose favour the disposition is alleged to have been made.

Sworn confirmation of the information

I ______ *(the above-named Applicant/ Respondent)*

of ______ make oath and confirm that the information given above is a full, frank, clear and accurate disclosure of my financial and other relevant circumstances.

Signed ______ Dated ______

Sworn by the above named [Applicant] [Respondent] at ______

on ______

before me ______

A [Solicitor] [Commissioner for Oaths] [Officer of a Court, appointed by the Judge to take Affidavits]

Address all communications to the Court Manager of the Court and quote the case number from page 1. If you do not quote this number, your correspondence may be returned.

The Court Office at

is open from 10a.m. to 4p.m. (4.30pm at the Principal Registry of the Family Division) on Monday to Friday only.

Sample Divorce Petition

Before completing this form, read carefully the attached **Notes for Guidance.**

In the **County Court*** *Delete as appropriate

In the Divorce Registry* **No.**

(1) On the day of [19] [20] the petitioner was lawfully married to (hereinafter called "the respondent") at

(2) The petitioner and respondent last lived together as husband and wife at

(3) The petitioner is domiciled in England and Wales, and is by occupation a and resides at and the respondent is by occupation a and resides at

(4) There are no children of the family now living *except*

(5) No other child, now living, has been born to the petitioner/respondent during the marriage (so far as is known to the petitioner) *except*

D8 (12.00) *Printed on behalf of The Court Service*

(6) There are or have been no other proceedings in any court in England and Wales or elsewhere with reference to the marriage (or to any child of the family) or between the petitioner and respondent with reference to any property of either or both of them *except*

(7) There are or have been no proceedings in the Child Support Agency with reference to the maintenance of any child of the family *except*

(8) There are no proceedings continuing in any country outside England or Wales which are in respect of the marriage or are capable of affecting its validity or subsistence *except*

(9) (This paragraph should be completed only if the petition is based on five years' separation.) No agreement or arrangement has been made or is proposed to be made between the parties for the support of the petitioner/respondent (and any child of the family) *except*

(10) The said marriage has broken down irretrievably.

(11)

You need this book first

(12) **Particulars**

Prayer

The petitioner therefore prays

(1) **The suit**

That the said marriage be dissolved

(2) **Costs**

That the   may be ordered to pay the costs of this suit

(3) **Ancillary relief**

That the petitioner may be granted the following ancillary relief:

(a) an order for maintenance pending suit

a periodical payments order

a secured provision order

a lump sum order

a property adjustment order

an order under section 24B, 25B or 25C of the Act of 1973 (Pension Sharing/ Attachment Order)

(b) **For the children**

a periodical payments order

a secured provision order

a lump sum order

a property adjustment order

Signed

The names and addresses of the persons to be served with this petition are:-

Respondent:-

Co-Respondent (adultery case only):-

The Petitioner's address for service is:-

Dated this   day of   20

Address all communications for the court to: The Court Manager, County Court,

The Court }
office at }

is open from 10 a.m. to 4 p.m. (4.30 p.m. at the Principal Registry of the Family Division) on Mondays to Fridays.

In the

*Delete as appropriate

County Court*

No.

In the Divorce Registry*

Between

Petitioner

and

Respondent

Divorce Petition

Full name and address of the petitioner or of solicitors if they are acting for the petitioner.

Divorce Petition
Notes for Guidance

Each of the notes below will help you to complete that paragraph in the divorce petition which has the same number as the note. You should not cross out any of the paragraphs numbered 1 to 12 unless the notes say that you should.

(1) You will find the information you need to complete this paragraph on your marriage certificate. You must explain any differences between the information given in your petition and that on your marriage certificate.

If either you or the respondent have changed your name(s) since the marriage took place you must explain this, for example by adding:

- name changed by deed poll,
- now known as.

Please give:

- the date of your marriage,
- your full name (the petitioner)
- the full name of your husband or wife (the respondent)
- the place of the marriage.

for example:

Where the marriage took place in a Register Office:

The Register Office, in the District of

....

in the County of ....

Where the marriage took place in a church:

.... Church, in the Parish of ....

in the County of ....

(2) Please give the last address at which you have lived with the respondent as husband and wife.

(3) Please give your occupation and current address and those of the respondent.

If either you or the respondent are not domiciled (that is, you or the respondent do not live permanently) in England and Wales please give the name of the countr(y)(ies) in which you are domiciled (in which you do live). Where both of you are domiciled (live permanently) outside England and Wales, add the following paragraph, if it applies:

"The petitioner (respondent) has been domiciled in England and Wales throughout the period of one year ending with the date of the presentation of the petition."

- You should give the address(es) where you and the respondent lived during that year and the length of time lived at each address.

(4) If there are no children of the family cross out the word "except". If there are any children of the family give:

- their full names (including surname),
- their date of birth, or if over 18 say so,
- if the child is over 16 but under 18, say if he or she is at school, or college,

  or

  is training for a trade, profession or vocation,

  or

  is working full time.

(5) If no other child has been born during the marriage you should cross out the word "except".

If you are the husband, cross out the word "petitioner" where it first appears in the paragraph, but do not cross out the words in brackets

If you are the wife, cross out the word "respondent", and cross out the words in brackets.

If there is a child give:

- the full name (including surname),
- the date of birth, or if over 18 say so.

If there is a dispute whether a living child is a child of the family please add a paragraph saying so.

(6) If there have not been any court proceedings in England and Wales concerning:

- your marriage,
- any child of the family,
- any property belonging to either you or the respondent

cross out the word "except".

D8 (Notes)

If there have been proceedings please give:

- the name of the court in which they took place,
- details of the order(s) which were made,
- if the proceedings were about your marriage say if you and the respondent resumed living together as husband and wife after the order was made.

(7) If there have not been any proceedings in the Child Support Agency concerning the maintenance of any child of the family, cross out the word "except".

If there have been any proceedings please give

- the date of any application to the Agency
- details of the assessment made.

(8) If there have been no proceedings in a court outside England and Wales which have affected the marriage, or may affect it, cross out the word "except".

If there are or have been proceedings please give:

- the name of the country and the court in which they are taking/have taken place,
- details of the order(s) made,
- if no order has yet been made, the date of any future hearing.

(9) If your petition is not based on five years' separation, cross out this paragraph.

If your petition is based on five year's separation but no agreement or arrangement has been made, cross out the word "except".

If your petition is based on five years, separation and an agreement or arrangement has been made with the respondent:

- about maintenance either for him or herself or for any child of the family,
- about the family property,

please give full details.

(10) If you are applying for a judicial separation please cross out this paragraph.

(11) Please write in, exactly as set out below, the paragraph (or paragraphs) upon which you intend to rely to prove that your marriage has irretrievably broken down.

***Please note:** You do not need to give the name of the person with whom the respondent has committed adultery unless you wish to claim costs against that person.*

(a) The respondent has committed adultery with a [man] [woman] and the petitioner finds it intolerable to live with the respondent.

or

The respondent has committed adultery [with (give the name) .... (called the co-respondent)] and the petitioner finds it intolerable to live with the respondent.

(b) The respondent has behaved in such a way that the petitioner cannot reasonably be expected to live with the respondent.

(c) The respondent has deserted the petitioner for a continuous period of at least two years immediately preceding the presentation of this petition.

(d) The parties to the marriage have lived apart for a continuous period of at least two years immediately preceding the presentation of the petition and the respondent consents to a decree being granted.

(e) The parties to the marriage have lived apart for a continuous period of at least five years immediately preceding the presentation of the petition.

Particulars

(12) This space is provided for you to give details of the allegations which you are using to prove the facts given in paragraph 11. In most cases one or two sentences will do.

(a) If you have alleged adultery give:

- the date(s) and place(s) where the adultery took place.

(b) If you have alleged unreasonable behaviour give:

- details of particular incidents, including dates, but it should not be necessary to give more than about half a dozen examples of the more serious incidents, including the most recent.

(c) If you have alleged desertion give:

- the date of desertion
- brief details of how the desertion came about.

(d) & (e) If you have alleged either two or five year's separation give:

- the date of separation,
- brief details of how the separation came about.

Prayer

The prayer of the petition is your request to the court. You should consider carefully the claims which you wish to make.

You should adapt the prayer to suit your claims.

(1) The suit

If you are asking for a judicial separation, cross out this paragraph and write in its place:

"That the petitioner may be judicially separated from the respondent".

(2) Costs

If you wish to claim that the respondent or co-respondent pay your costs you must do so in your petition.

It is not possible to make a claim after a decree has been granted.

If you do wish to claim costs write in respondent, or co-respondent, or both, as appropriate.

If you do not wish to claim costs, cross out this paragraph.

(3) Ancillary relief

If you wish to apply for any of these orders, complete paragraph 3 by deleting those orders you do not require.

You are advised to see a solicitor if you are unsure about which order(s) you require.

If you cross out this paragraph, or any part of it, and later change your mind, you will first have to ask the court's permission before any application can be made. Permission cannot be granted after re-marriage.

If you apply in the prayer for an order you must complete Form A when you are ready to proceed with your application.

If you are asking for a property adjustment order, give the address of the property concerned.

If you are asking for a pension sharing or attachment order, give details of the order you require.

You can apply to the court for ancillary relief for children if you are asking for one or more of the following:

- a lump sum payment,
- * settlement of property,
- * transfer of property,
- * secured periodical payments,
- financial provision for a stepchild or stepchildren of the respondent.

** These orders can only be made in the High Court or a county court.*

- periodical payments when either the child or,

  the person with care of the child, or

  the absent parent of the child is **not** habitually resident in the United Kingdom,
- periodical payments in addition to child support maintenance paid under a Child Support Agency assessment,
- periodical payments to meet expenses arising from a child's disability,
- periodical payments to meet expenses incurred by a child in being educated or training for work.

If none of the above applies to you, you should make an application for child maintenance to the Child Support Agency; the court cannot make an order for child maintenance in your case. A leaflet about the Child Support Agency is available from any court office.

If you are not sure whether the court can hear your application please ask a member of the court staff. A leaflet 'I want to apply for a financial order' is also available.

Finally, do not forget to

- sign and date the petition,
- give the name(s) and personal address(es) of the person(s) to be served with the petition,
- bring or send your marriage certificate and fee to the court,
- complete a Statement of Arrangements if there are children of the family.

Arrangements for Children

If you consider that the court will need to:

- determine where the child(ren) should live (a Residence Order),
- determine with whom the child(ren) should have contact (a Contact Order),
- make a Specific Issue Order,
- make a Prohibited Steps Order,

you must apply for the order form C2.
You may enclose the completed form with your petition or submit it later. If you wish to apply for any of these orders, or any other orders which may be available to you under part I or II of the Children Act 1989, you are advised to see a solicitor.

The Court will only make an order if it considers that an order will be better for the child(ren) than no order.

All forms and leaflets are available from your Court.

Printed on behalf of The Court Service

Statement of Arrangements for Children

Statement of Arrangements for Children

In the	County Court
Petitioner	
Respondent	
No. of matter *(always quote this)*	

To the Petitioner

You must complete this form
If you or the respondent have any children • under 16
or • over 16 not under 18 if they are at school or college or are training for a trade, profession or vocation.

Please use black ink.
Please complete Parts I, II and III.

Before you issue a petition for divorce try to reach agreement with your husband/wife over the proposals for the children's future. There is space for him/her to sign at the end of this form if agreement is reached.

If your husband/wife does not agree with the proposals he/she will have an opportunity at a later stage to state why he/she does not agree and will be able to make his/her own proposals.

You should take or send the completed form, signed by you (and, if agreement is reached, by your husband/wife) together with a copy to the court when you issue your petition.

Please refer to the explanatory notes issued regarding completion of the prayer of the petition if you are asking the court to make any order regarding the children.

The Court will only make an order if it considers that an order will be better for the child(ren) than no order.

If you wish to apply for any of the orders which may be available to you under Part I or II of the Children Act 1989 you are advised to see a solicitor.

You should obtain legal advice from a solicitor or, alternatively, from an advice agency. Addresses of solicitors and advice agencies can be obtained from the Yellow Pages and the Solicitors Regional Directory which can be found at Citizens Advice Bureaux, Law Centres and any local library.

To the Respondent

The petitioner has completed Part I, II and III of this form which will be sent to the Court at the same time that the divorce petition is filed.

Please read all parts of the form carefully.

If you agree with the arrangements and proposals for the children you should sign Part IV of the form. Please use black ink. You should return the form to the petitioner, or his/her solicitor.

If you do not agree with all or some of the arrangements of proposals you will be given the opportunity of saying so when the divorce petition is served on you.

Part 1 - Details of the children

Please read the instructions for boxes 1, 2 and 3 before you complete this section

1. Children of both parties

(Give details only of any children born to you and the Respondent or adopted by you both)

	Forenames	Surname	Date of birth
(i)			
(ii)			
(iii)			
(iv)			
(v)			

2. Other children of the family

(Give details of any other children treated by both of you as children of the family: for example your own or the Respondent's)

	Forenames	Surname	Date of birth	Relationship to Yourself	Relationship to Respondent
(i)					
(ii)					
(iii)					
(iv)					
(v)					

3. Other children who are not children of the family

(Give details of any children born to you or the Respondent that have not been treated as children of the family or adopted by you both)

	Forenames	Surname	Date of birth
(i)			
(ii)			
(iii)			
(iv)			
(v)			

Part II - Arrangements for the children of the family

This part of the form must be completed. Give details for each child if arrangements are different. (if necessary, continue on another sheet and attach it to this form)

4. Home details *(please tick the appropriate boxes)*

(a) The addresses at which the children now live

(b) Give details of the number of living rooms, bedrooms, etc. at the addresses in (a)

(c) Is the house rented or owned and by whom?

Is the rent or any mortgage being regularly paid? ☐ No ☐ Yes

(d) Give the names of all other persons living with the children including your husband/wife if he/she lives there. State their relationship to the children.

(e) Will there be any change in these arrangements? ☐ No ☐ Yes *(please give details)*

3

5. Education and training details

(please tick the appropriate boxes)

(a) Give the names of the school, college or place of training attended by each child.	
(b) Do the children have any special educational needs?	☐ No ☐ Yes *(please give details)*
(c) Is the school, college or place of training, fee-paying?	☐ No ☐ Yes *(please give details of how much the fees are per term / year)*
Are fees being regularly paid?	☐ No ☐ Yes *(please give details)*
(d) Will there be any change in these arrangements?	☐ No ☐ Yes *(please give details)*

6. Childcare details *(please tick the appropriate boxes)*

(a) Which parent looks after the children from day to day? If responsibility is shared, please give details		
(b) Does that parent go out to work?	☐ No ☐ Yes	*(please give details of his/her hour of work)*
(c) Does someone look after the children when the parent is not there?	☐ No ☐ Yes	*(please give details)*
(d) Who looks after the children during school holidays?		
(e) Will there be any change in these arrangements?	☐ No ☐ Yes	*(please give details)*

7. Maintenance *(please tick the appropriate boxes)*

(a) Does your husband/wife pay towards the upkeep of the children? If there is another source of maintenance, please specify.	☐ No ☐ Yes	*(please give details of how much)*
(b) Is the payment made under a court order?	☐ No ☐ Yes	*(please give details, including the name of the court and the case number)*
(c) Is the payment following an assessment by the Child Support Agency?	☐ No ☐ Yes	*(please give details of how much)*
(d) Has maintenance for the children been agreed?	☐ No ☐ Yes	
(e) If not, will you be applying for:		
• a child maintenance order from the court	☐ No ☐ Yes	
• child support maintenance through the Child Support Agency?	☐ No ☐ Yes	

5

8. Details for contact with the children

(please tick the appropriate boxes)

(a) Do the children see your husband/wife?

☐ No ☐ Yes *(please give details of how often and where)*

(b) Do the children ever stay with your husband/wife?

☐ No ☐ Yes *(please give details of how much)*

(c) Will there be any change to these arrangements?

☐ No ☐ Yes *(please give details of how much)*

Please give details of the proposed arrangements for contact and residence.

6

9. Details of health *(please tick the appropriate boxes)*

(a) Are the children generally in good health?

☐ No ☐ Yes *(please give details of any serious disability or chronic illness)*

(b) Do the children have any special health needs?

☐ No ☐ Yes *(please give details of the care needed and how it is to be provided)*

10. Details of Care and other court proceedings *(please tick the appropriate boxes)*

(a) Are the children in the care of a local authority, or under the supervision of a social worker or probation officer?

☐ No ☐ Yes *(please give details including any court proceedings)*

(b) Are any of the children on the Child Protection Register?

☐ No ☐ Yes *(please give details of the local authority and the date of registration)*

(c) Are there or have there been any proceedings in any court involving the children, for example adoption, custody/residence, access/contact, wardship, care, supervision or maintenance?

(You need not include any Child Support Agency proceedings here)

☐ No ☐ Yes *(please give details and send a copy of any order to the court)*

Part III To the Petitioner

Conciliation

If you and your husband/wife do not agree about arrangements for the child(ren), would you agree to discuss the matter with a Conciliator and your husband/wife? ☐ No ☐ Yes

Declaration

I declare that the information I have given is correct and complete to the best of my knowledge.

Signed . . . . (Petitioner)

Date: . . . .

Part IV To the Respondent

I agree with the arrangements and proposals contained in Part I and II of this form.

Signed . . . . (Respondent)

Date: . . . .

Application for Remission of Fees

Application for a fee exemption or remission (Notes)

You must fill in one of these forms for each fee which you would like the court to remit, or exempt you from paying.

1 Information about fees

The county court office has leaflets which deal with your type of case and which contain information about fees. For instance, the leaflets *About Divorce, Children and the Family Courts* and *County Court Fees*.

The court office will tell you which leaflets you need. The leaflets are free.

2 Before you fill in the form

Read through it carefully because some of the questions may not apply to you.

3 When you fill in the form

You must fill in parts 1 and 2. Then follow the instruction beside your answer to question 2f.

4 After you have filled in the application form

Take the application form, or post it, to the office of the court which will deal with your case.

Note 4A: Other documents

You must enclose the form which you would like the court to issue (for instance, a divorce petition or a claim).
You will also have to provide evidence to support the information which you give on the application form. The evidence is explained in Note 4B, Note 4C and Note 4D.

Note 4B: Evidence of legal assistance

If your case is a family case, and you are receiving legal advice and assistance from a solicitor under the C10 (Green Form) Scheme (under the Legal Aid Act 1988), you **must** provide evidence that you are receiving that help. The court may ask your solicitor to confirm the evidence.

Note 4C: Evidence of benefits

If you are receiving :

Working Families Tax Cre
or Income Support
or Income-based Job Seeker's Allowance
or Disabled Person's Tax Credit,

you **must** provide evidence that you are receiving the benefit.

The evidence must be a recent document such as a letter from the Benefits Agency or your current benefit book. If you are receiving Working Families Tax Credit or Disabled Person's Tax Credit, you must provide your notice of award from the Inland Revenue.
You may enclose a photocopy of your evidence if you post the application form to the court.

Note 4D: Evidence of financial details

If you are **not** receiving :

Working Families Tax Credit
or Income Support
or Income-based Job Seeker's Allowance
or Disabled Person's Tax Credit
or legal advice and assistance under the C10 (Green Form) Scheme in a **family** case,

you must fill in parts 3, 4, 5, 6, 7, 8 and 9. You will have to provide evidence to support the financial details which you put in those parts of the form.

5 What will happen next

The court will consider the application and tell you the fee to pay (if any).

If you have to pay a fee, you may pay by cash or cheque. If you pay by cheque please make it payable to *HMPG*.

If you pay by cheque and it is dishonoured, the application, and the court proceedings related to it, will be stopped until payment has been made. That may mean that you have to pay additional costs.
The Court Service will always pursue recovery of dishonoured cheques.

Application for a fee exemption or remission

For the court's use only

In the ______ County Court

Reference Number

Evidence for automatic exemption? Yes ☐ No ☐
Benefits at Note 4c, or C10/Green Form if family case

Remission granted? Yes ☐ No ☐

Court fee £

Amount exempted or remitted £

Signed

Date

Grade

1 About the case

a Name of Claimant or Petitioner — *in BLOCK LETTERS*

b Name of Defendant or Respondent — *in BLOCK LETTERS*

c The **Case Number**, if you know it

d The title of the form which you would like the court to issue :
See Note 4A

2 About you

a Surname or family name — *in BLOCK LETTERS*

b Other names — *in BLOCK LETTERS*

c Title — Mr ☐ Mrs ☐ Miss ☐ Ms ☐

d Address

e Marital status — Married Single Other

f Are you receiving legal advice under the C10 (Green Form) Scheme, in a **family** case?
*If you answer **Yes**, please give your solicitor's name, reference, address and daytime telephone number.*
See Note 4B

No ☐ Go to question 2g.

Yes ☐ Put your solicitor's details in the boxes below. Then go to part 9.

Solicitor's name ______ Ref.

Address

Telephone number (daytime)

g Are you receiving :

Working Families Tax Credit

or Income Support

or Income-based Job Seeker's Allowance

or Disabled Person's Tax Credit?

No ☐ Go to part 3. *See Note 4D.*

Yes ☐ Read Note 4C. Then go to part 9, and sign and date the Declaration.

EX160 Application for a fee exemption or remission (10.99)

Printed on behalf of The Court Service

3 Dependants (people who you look after financially)

The number of children aged : under 11 | 11-15 | 16-17 | 18

Other dependants
Give details

4 Employment

Are you employed? No Yes Type of employment

Are you self-employed? No Yes Type of employment

Are you unemployed? No Yes How long have you been unemployed?

Are you a pensioner? No Yes

5 Your property

Do you live :
✓*one box*

in your own property? in lodgings? in rented property?

in property which you own jointly with someone else?

in other property? Please explain
for instance, with your parents)

6 Your savings

Give an amount for each type of savings. If you do not have one of the types shown, put NIL.

Bank account (Current)	£	Premium Bonds	£
Bank account (Deposit)	£	Stocks and Shares *(or both)*	£
Building Society Accounts (1)	£	National Savings Investments	£
(2)	£	Other savings which are:	£

7 Your usual monthly income

Give an amount for each type of income. If you do not have one of the types of income shown, put NIL. Add up the amounts and put the sum in the **Total income each month** *box.*

Your usual take home pay	£	Child Benefit	£
Your partner's usual take home pay *(if applicable)*	£	Other benefit(s) which are:	£
Income from other people who live with you	£		£
Your pension(s) *(put the total)*	£	**Total income each month**	£

8 Your usual monthly expenses

Give an amount for each type of expense. If you do not have one of the expenses, put NIL. Add up the amounts and put the sum in the **Total expenses each month** *box.*

Rent or Mortgage	£	Child care	£
Council Tax *(give the amount you actually pay)*	£	Travelling expenses	£
Water and Sewerage charges	£	Food and household essentials	£
Maintenance and Child Support	£	Court fines	£
Electricity	£	Clothing	£
Gas, coal and oil	£	Other expenses which are :	£
Telephone	£		£
TV rent and licence	£	**Total expenses each month**	£

9 Declaration

I declare that the information which I have given is true to the best of my knowledge and belief. I understand that I may be asked to provide documents as evidence to support my statements and that my application will not proceed if I do not provide the evidence. I also understand that my application will be refused if I have not disclosed any relevant facts in this form.

Signed Date

EX160 Application for a fee exemption or remission (10.99) *Printed on behalf of The Court Service*

Application for Bailiff Service of Petition

Request for servicd by Court Bailiff

FAMILY PROCEEDINGS RULES **COUNTY COURT***

PRINCIPAL REGISTRY*

*Delete and/or complete as appropriate

No. of Matter

Between Petitioner

and Respondent

I hereby request that the Respondent be served by the court bailiff with the Petition in this matter.

The full name of the Respondent is:

The address (in England/Wales) at which bailiff service should be attempted is:-

I enclose/do not have a recent photograph of the Respondentl

Signed:

(Solicitors for the) Petitioner

Address:

Telephone:

Date:

1999 Edition

6.1999 MM

Divorce 96

Notice of Issue of Petition

No. of matter:

Between Petitioner

and Respondent

and Co-Respondent

The matter has been given the above number. The number must be put on all documents filed with the court and on all correspondence (the address of the court is at the bottom of this form)

- The petition was issued on the:
- A copy of the petition was posted to the respondent on:
- If you do not receive a copy of the completed acknowledgement of service(s) within 14 days from the date of posting you may**:

A Apply to the court bailiff to personally serve the petition (Solicitors may attempt service themselves). To apply, you should send or bring to the court:

(a) Completed form D89 (Report for bailiff service) which may be obtained from the court office

(b) A photograph or written description of the respondent (or co-respondent)

* (c) A copy of your petition (and a copy of the statement of arrangements for children)

* (d) A cheque or postal order for £10.00 made payable to "H.M. Paymaster General" and crossed

B Apply to the court ex-parte on affidavit for the District Judge to consider whether the petition may be deemed to have been served in accordance with the Family Proceedings Rules. This application will attract a "fee of £30.00}.

C Apply to the court ex-parte on affidavit for the District Judge to consider whether the directions should be given.
This application will attract a* fee of £30.00

**These will not be required if you are being advised under the green form scheme*

*** For further guidance see D184 Leaflet 2 "I want to get a divorce – what do I do?"*

Please note that you will not receive a further notification (other than the acknowledgment of service) unless the petition is returned to the court by the Post Office.

To The Petitioner('s Solicitor) **Dated:**

Acknowledgement of Service

No. of matter:

Between	Petitioner
and	Respondent
and	Co-Respondent

- If you intend to instruct a solicitor to act for you, give him this form immediately
- Read carefully the Notice of Proceedings before answering the following questions
- Pleae complete using black ink.

1.	Have you received the petition for divorce delivered with this form?
2.	On which date and at what address did you receive it?
3.	Are you the person named as the Respondent in the petition?
4.	Do you intend to defend the case?
5.	(In the case of a petition alleging adultery) Do you admit the adultery alleged in the petition?
6.	Even if you do not intend to defend the case do you object to paying the costs of the proceedings? If so, on what grounds?
7.	(a) Have you received a copy of the Statement of Arrangements for the child(ren)? (b) Have you received a copy of the Statement of Arrangements? (the date beside the Petitioner's signature at Part 3) (c) Do you agree with the proposals in that Statement of Arrangements **Notes** If NO you may file a written statment of your views on the present and the proposed arrangements for the children. It would help if you sent that statement to the court office with this form. You can get a form from the court office.
8.	(In the case of proceedings relating to a polygamous marriage) If you have any wife/husband in addition to the petitioner who is not mentioned in the petition, what is the name and address of each such wife/husband and the date and place of your marriage to her/him?

9(a) **You must complete this part if**

or

- you answered **Yes** to **Question 7(c)**

or

- you do **not** have a solicitor acting for you

Signed: Date:

Address for service*

*Note: If you are acting on your own you should also put your place of residence, or if you do not reside in England or Wales the address of a place in England or Wales to which documents may be sent to you. If you subsequently wish to change your address for service, you must notify the Court.

9(b) I am/We are acting for the Respondent in this matter.

Signed: Solicitor for the Respondent

Date:

Address for service:

Note: If your client answered **Yes** to **Question 5** or **Question 7(c)** your client must sign and date at 9(a).

Address all communications to the Court Manager **and quote the case number.**

Acknowledgement of Service – Respondent spouse

F.P. Rule 2.9(5)(Form M6) **D10(1**

ADDENDUM TO THE ACKNOWLEDGEMENT OF SERVICE – Respondents only.

(In respect of a petition issued on or after 1st March 2001)

The following Questions 1A, 1B and 1C, as well as all questions on the form of acknowledgement of service, MUST be answered:

1A. Are there any proceedings continuing in any country outside England and Wales, which rela the marriage or are capable of affecting its validity or subsistence?
If so, please provide the following information:

(a) particulars of the proceedings;

(b) the date when they were begun;

(c) the names of the parties;

(d) the date or expected date of any trial in the proceedings, and

(e) such other facts as may be relevant to the question whether the proceedings on the petition should be stayed under Article 11 of the Council Regulation.

1B. In which country are you –
(a) Domiciled?

(b) Habitually resident?

(c) Of which country are you a national?

1C. Do you agree with the statement of the petitioner as to the grounds of jurisdiction set out in the petition? If not, please state the grounds on which you disagree with the statement of the petitioner.

Application for Directions for Trial

In the **County Court**

No of matter

Between Petitioner

and Respondent

and Co-respondent

Application for directions for trial (Special Procedure) *F.P. Rules 2.24*

The petitioner applies to the District Judge for directions for the trial of this undefended cause by entering it in the Special Procedure List.

The petitioner's affidavit of evidence is lodged with this application.

Signed [Solicitor for] the petitioner

Dated

If you write to the Court please address your letters to "The Court Manager" and quote the **No. of the matter** at the top of this form.

The Court Office is at

and is open from 10am to 4pm on Monday to Friday.

D84-w3 (12.98)

Certificate of Entitlement to a Divorce

NO:

IN THE .... County Court

BETWEEN Petitioner

AND Respondent

Certificate of entitlement to a decree

F.P. Rules 2.36(1)

The Court certifies that the petitioner has sufficiently proved the contents of the petition and is entitled to a decree of divorce on the grounds of the Respondent's unreasonable behaviour.

Date:

Take notice that the Court has fixed the at for the pronouncement of a decree by a District Judge sitting at Ipswich County Court, 8 Arcade Street, Ipswich, IP1 1EJ

Note: Unless the decree of any of the orders is opposed, it is unnecessary for any party to appear at Court for the pronouncement.

The court office at Ipswich County Court, 8 Arcade Street, Ipswich, IP1 1EJ is open from 10:00am until 4:00pm on Mondays to Fridays. Tel 01473 214256 Please address all communications to the Court Manager quoting the number at the top right hand corner of this form.
Printed By ECOATES

D84A Notice of Decree Nisi date

You need this book first

Sample of Decree Nisi (behaviour)

(Note that other decrees will be amended differently)

NO:

IN THE .... County Court

BETWEEN Petitioner

AND Respondent

Before District Judge sitting at County Court

On the

The Judge held that

the respondent has behaved in such a way that the petitioner cannot reasonably be expected to live with the respondent,

that the marriage solemnised on

at

between the Petitioner

and the Respondent

has broken down irretrievably and decreed that the said marriage be dissolved unless sufficient cause be shown to the Court within six weeks from the making of this decree why such decree should not be made absolute.

Notes

This is not the final decree. Application for the final decree (decree absolute) must be made to the court. (*For guidance see leaflet D187 "I have a decree nisi – what must I do next"*)

Appeals: showing cause why this decree nisi should not be made final (absolute) is not an appeal against the decree nisi.

*If the decree was pronounced by a district judge and the respondent wishes to appeal, he or she must serve notice of appeal and set down the appeal at this court within 14 days of the date of the decree nisi.

*If the decree nisis was pronounced by a judge and the respondent wishes to appeal, he or she must serve notice of appeal and set down the appeal at the Court of Appeal within 4 weeks of the date of the decree nisi.

The court office at Ipswich County Court, 8 Arcade Street, Ipswich, IP1 1EJ is open from 10:00am until 4:00pm on Mondays to Fridays. Tel 01473 214256 Please address all communications to the Court Manager quoting the number at the top right hand corner of this form.
Printed By ECOATES
Printed by R CHENERY

D29 Family Man1 D29 Report

Application for Decree Absolute

Notice of Application for Decree Nisi to be made Absolute.
(Form M8, Appendix 1, F.P.R. 191)

FAMILY PROCEEDINGS RULES **IN THE** **COUNTY COURT* PRINCIPAL REGISTRY***

*Complete and/or delete as appropriate. If proceeding in a District Registry, delete both headings and insert "in the High Court of Justice, Family Division District Registry".

No. of Matter

Between Petitioner

and Respondent

TAKE NOTICE that the Petitioner

applies for the decree nisi pronounced in his (her) favour on the

day of to be made absolute.

Dated this day of

Signed:

(Solicitors for the) Petitioner

of

Address all communications for the Court to: The Court Manager, County Court*

(or to the Principal Registry, First Avenue House, 42-49 High Holborn, London, WC1V 6NP) quoting the number in the top right-hand corner of this form. The Court Office is open from 10 a.m. till 4 p.m. (4.30 p.m. at t he Principal Registry) on Mondays to Fridays only.

DIV 100/1

You need this book first

No.of Matter

IN THE HIGH COURT OF JUSTICE

FAMILY DIVISION

(Divorce)

Between

and

NOTICE

of Application for Decree Nisi
to be made Absolute

1999 Edition
6.1999 MM

DIV 100/2

Divorce 100

Sample of Decree Absolute

NO:

IN THE .... County Court

BETWEEN Petitioner

AND Respondent

Referring to the decree made in this cause on the whereby it was decreed that the marriage solemnised on the

between the Petitioner

and the Respondent

be dissolved unless sufficient cause be shown to the Court within six weeks from the making thereof why the said decree should not be made absolute, and no such cause having been shown, it is hereby certified that the said decree was on the , made final and absolute and that the said marriage was thereby dissolved.

Dated:

Notes:

1. Divorce affects inheritance under a will

   Where a will has already been made by either party to the marriage then, by virtue of section 18A of the Wills Act 1937:
   (a) any provisions of the will appointing the former spouse executor or trustee or conferring a power of appointment on the former spouse shall take effect as if the former spouse had died on the date on which the marriage is disolved unless a contrary intention appears in the will:

   (b) any property which, or an interest in which, is devised or bequeathed to the former spouse shall pass as if the former spouse had died on the date on which the marriage is dissolved unless a contrary intention appears in the will.

2. Divorce affects the appointment of a guardian.

   Unless a contrary intention is shown in the instrument of appointment, any appointment under section 5(3) or 5(4) of the Children Act 1989 by one spouse of his or her former spouse as guardian is, by virtue of section 6 of that Act, deemed to have been revoked at the date of the dissolution of the marriage.

The court office at Ipswich County Court, 8 Arcade Street, Ipswich, IP1 1EJ is open from 10:00am until 4:00pm on Mondays to Fridays. Tel 01473 214256 Please address all communications to the Court Manager quoting the number at the top right hand corner of this form.
Printed By ECOATES

D37 Decree of Absolute (Divorce)

Form E

(Financial Statement in Ancillary Relief Proceedings)

Notes for guidance

About these notes:

- They explain some of the terms used in Form E that may be unfamiliar to you.
- The most important notes are in **BOLD**. Please do not ignore them.
- There is also checklist at the end of these notes to tell you which documents you will need to attach to Form E.

These notes are only a guide to help you complete Form E. If you require further help you should speak to a solicitor, Citizens Advice Bureau, legal advice centre or law centre. Public funding of your legal costs may be available from the Community Legal Service Fund. **Please note, while court staff will help on procedural matters, they cannot offer any legal advice.**

Introduction

If you or your spouse apply to the court for a financial order, both you and the other person **must** complete a separate Form E. The purpose of the form is to enable you to provide the court with full details of your financial arrangements.

You must send your completed Form E to the court and a copy to the other party, no later than 35 days before the date of the First Appointment. The date of the First Appointment can be found on Form C (Notice of a first appointment) which will be sent to you by the court.

You should be aware that the court might make an order for costs against you if you do not follow the deadlines for filing Form E.

If you and the other person have agreed about the financial matters there is no need for either of you to complete a Form E. Your agreement (sometimes known as a consent application) should be submitted to the Court prior to the First Appointment.

Part 1 General Information (Pages 2-3)

Section 1.6: The court can provide you with these dates if you are unsure. Please quote your case number when asking for details.

Section 1.11: You only need to provide details if you or your child(ren) are suffering from any form of physical or mental disability. The court does not need to know about minor ailments.

Section 1.13: You need to supply details of any Child Support Agency assessments, agreements or court orders in respect of child support. Also, if an application has been made to the Child Support Agency but not decided let the court know the result of the application, when it has been decided. If you need help to complete this section you can contact the National Enquiry Line of the Child Support Agency (Telephone 0845 7133133).

Section 1.15: You should give details of any other previous or current court cases between you and the other person. (It would also help the court if you provided brief details about the nature of these proceedings e.g. residence/contact in respect of the children).

Part 2 Financial Details (Pages 4-14)

Section 2.1: You need to tell the court if you own or part own the matrimonial home and how much you think it is currently worth*. Details of the Land Registry title number and of the balance outstanding on any mortgage can be obtained by contacting the company with whom you have your mortgage. You can also obtain your Land Registry Title number from HM Land Registry, Lincoln's Inn Fields, London, WC2A 3PH (Telephone 020 7917 8888).

The box headed 'Total current value of your beneficial interest' refers to the amount you feel that you are owed after deducting the outstanding balance of your mortgage from the sale price of your home.

*** If you have obtained a valuation on your property within the last six months you will need to attach a copy to form E.**

Section 2.11: "Realisable assets" are those which can easily be converted into cash.

Section 2.12: You need to list any debts/bills that are currently outstanding.

Section 2.13: For further information about Capital Gains Tax you can contact the Inland Revenue who produce a free booklet called "Capital Gains Tax - an introduction". (Reference number - CGT1). Telephone 0845 9000404. You may want to seek legal and/or financial advice to answer this question.

Section 2.16: You will need to provide the court with details of all your pension benefits, including those relating to your present and/or a previous job and/or resulting from membership of a personal (i.e. privately arranged) pension scheme.

If you have been provided with a valuation of your pension rights or benefits by the person responsible for your pension scheme you must attach a copy of it to Form E. (You may only use a valuation if it will not be more than a year old at the date of the first appointment). If you do not have this information, or the valuation you have will be more than a year old, you should write to the person responsible for your pension scheme and ask them to provide you with an up to date valuation. A copy of your letter requesting the valuation should be attached to Form E together with any reply from the pension scheme letting you know when this information will be available. If you have more than one pension plan or scheme you must provide this information for each one.

The administrators of your scheme will be able to provide the information requested. **It may help to send the administrators a copy of page 10 of Form E.**

If you have an occupational pension scheme your employer will be able to provide you with the name and address of your pension administrators.

If you have a personal pension scheme (i.e. privately arranged) you should contact the administrators directly. If you are unsure of the details of your pension scheme you can contact:

The Pensions Schemes Registry
PO Box 1NN
Newcastle Upon Tyne
NE99 1NN

You can request a forecast of your potential state pension by filling in form BR19 (available from social security offices) and sending it to:

Benefits Agency
RFPA Unit
Pensions and Overseas Benefit Directorate
Newcastle Upon Tyne
NE98 1YX

> **Note:** Please make certain that you provide the court with your National Insurance Number. If the Form E that you are using does not include a box for this, please write this information in below the 'Name and Address of your pension scheme, plan or policy').

Section 2.17: "unrealisable assets" are those which cannot be easily converted into cash. For example, shares in a family business or being the minority owner of a property.

A solicitor will be able to advise you whether an asset is realisable or not. If in doubt, the asset should be mentioned in this section and the judge will decide.

Section 2.18: As well as completing this section, you must also attach copies of your last three payslips and your P60 for the most recently completed financial year.

Section 2.25: This is a quick summary of the information you have provided previously in Part 2 of Form E. To complete it, you will need to refer back to each section in Part 2 again and only note the figure in the box with an alphabetical reference number next to it. For example, you will find the figure for (A) on page 4, in section 2.1.

Part 3 Requirements (Pages 15-16)

Section 3.1: Under the box headed "Income needs of yourself" you need to add the weekly, monthly or annual cost of each item. It should include, for example, finance payments where a car or household goods are being purchased on credit. *(If you run out of space when completing this section, please continue on a separate sheet of paper and attach to Form E, clearly numbering the section they refer to e.g. section 2.3 cont.)*

Section 3.2: You should also include in this section details of any items you hope to buy in the near future. For example, the reasonable cost of buying a new car or house.

Part 4 Other Information (Pages 17-18)

Section 4.2: The term "standard of living" invites you to express your own view or opinion. Try to give details of the kind of lifestyle you and the family enjoyed during your marriage. For example, the number of holidays you took over the course of a year.

Section 4.3: The term "contribution" does not solely refer to financial contributions and you can include the fact that you looked after the family home and cared for the family unit.

Section 4.6: If you have remarried or are living with another person (or intend to) you will need to complete this section. It is important that the court making the decision has as complete a picture of the available finances as possible.

Part 5 Order sought (Pages 19-20)

You may wish to seek legal advice to answer the questions in this part of Form E. Public funding of your legal costs may be available from the Community Legal Service Fund.

Section 5.2: You must clearly identify what the asset is. For example, if it is a property you will need to write in the address.

Section 5.4: An 'Avoidance of Disposition Order' is an order that the court can make to set aside or overturn a transaction that has already taken place (or that you believe is about to take place) e.g. a sale/mortgage of land or other asset. You might consider this transaction to be a step intended by the other party to deprive you of the benefit of sharing in it, or may have the effect of reducing the assets available for distribution between you.

Sworn confirmation of the information you have provided in Form E is true

This section must be completed. You have to confirm either by swearing on oath or by affirming that the information you have provided is a **full, frank, clear and accurate disclosure** of your financial and other relevant circumstances. You can do this either before a member of the court staff (this is free) or before a solicitor or commissioner for oaths (there will be a fee for this).

Please note – any copy documents that you wish to attach to Form E will need to be sworn as an exhibit or attachment to Form E. You should also indicate to which section of Form E these copy documents refer.

Checklist

Now that you have completed Form E please ensure that copies of the following items, relevant to your application, are attached.

(You should not attach original documents but keep them available for inspection by the other party and the Court)

- A recent mortgage statement *(see sections 2.1 and 2.2)*
- A valuation, if you have obtained one within the last 6 months *(see sections 2.1 and 2.2)*
- Bank statements in respect of the past 12 months, for each bank account you have listed *(see section 2.3)*
- Life insurance surrender value quotations *(see section 2.5)*
- A copy of the last 2 years business accounts for all your business interests. *(see section 2.14)*
- Any other documents that may affect your valuation of your business interests. *(see section 2.14)*
- A valuation of your rights or benefits under a pension scheme or plan, or a letter requesting such a valuation. Separate information must be provided for each scheme or plan you have listed. *(see section 2.16)*
- Your last 3 payslips *(see section 2.18)*
- Your P60 for the most recently completed financial year *(see section 2.18)*
- Accounts for the last 2 completed accounting years *(see section 2.20)*

(If you are unable to attach any copy documents to Form E when you file it you MUST add a short note to Form E explaining why you were unable to attach the copy document)

Form E (Notes) Guidance notes for Form E (12.00) *Printed on behalf of The Court Service*

Notice of Allegation in Proceedings for Ancillary Relief

In the	
*[County Court] *[Principal Registry of the Family Division]	
Case No. *Always quote this*	
Applicant's Solicitor's reference	
Respondent's Solicitor's reference	

*(*delete as appropriate)*

The marriage of **and**

Take Notice that

The following statement has been filed in proceedings for ancillary relief:

Signed: Dated:

[Applicant / Respondent/Solicitor for the Applicant / Respondent]

If you wish to be heard on any matter affecting you in these proceedings you may intervene by applying to the Court for directions regarding:

- the filing and service of pleadings
- the conduct of further proceedings

You must apply for directions **within seven days** after you receive this Notice. The period of seven days includes the day you receive it.

The court office at

is open between 10 am and 4 pm (4.30pm at the Principal Registry of the Family Division) Monday to Friday. When corresponding with the court, please address forms or letters to the Court Manager and quote the case number. If you do not do so, your correspondence may be returned.

Form F Notice of allegation in proceedings for ancillary relief (6.2000) *Printed on behalf of the Court Service*

Ancillary Relief Costs Estimate of *[Applicant] *[Respondent]

In the	
*[County Court] *[Principal Registry of the Family Division]	
Case No. *Always quote this*	
Applicant's Solicitor's reference	
Respondent's Solicitor's reference	

*(*delete as appropriate)*

Click here to clear all fields

The marriage of and

PART 1

	Prescribed rates for publicly funded services £	Indemnity Rate £
1. Ancillary relief solicitor's costs *(including VAT)* including costs of the current hearing, and any previous solicitor's costs.		
2. Disbursements *(include VAT, if appropriate, and any incurred by previous solicitors)*		
3. All Counsel's fees *(including VAT)*		
TOTAL	£0.00	£0.00

PART 2

4. Add any private client costs previously incurred *(In publicly funded cases only)*		
5. GRAND TOTAL	£0.00	£0.00

PART 3

6. State what has been paid towards the total at 5 above		
7. Amount of any contributions paid by the funded client towards their publicly funded services		

NB. If you are publicly funded and might be seeking an order for costs against the other party complete both rates.

Dated

The court office at

is open between 10 am and 4 pm (4.30pm at the Principal Registry of the Family Division) Monday to Friday. When corresponding with the court, please address forms or letters to the Court Manager and quote the case number. If you do not do so, your correspondence may be returned.

Form H Costs Estimate (12.00) *Printed on behalf of The Court Service*

Sample letters

Letter to Court enclosing Divorce Petition

Your address

Date

Chief Clerk

.... County Court

[Address of County Court]

Dear Sir

Divorce

I am the Petitioner in this matter and I enclose:

Marriage Certificate

Divorce Petition x 3 [x 4 if you are citing a co-respondent]

Statement of Arrangements for Children x 3 [*If your partner has already signed the Statement, add 'signed by the Respondent' here]*

Cheque for £150 *or* Application for Remission of Fees.

Thank you for your assistance in this matter.

Yours faithfully

Letter to Court enclosing Application for Directions for Trial and Affidavit

Your address

Date

Chief Clerk

.... County Court

[Address of County Court]

Case no: [you will have a case number by now: insert it here]

Dear Sir

Divorce

I am the Petitioner in this matter and I am now applying for Directions for Trial. I enclose:

Application for Directions for trial

Affidavit

Thank you for your assistance in this matter.

Yours faithfully

Letter to Court asking for Petition to be served by Court Bailiff

Your address

Date

Chief Clerk

.... County Court

[Address of County Court]

Case no: [if you have one, insert it here]

Dear Sir

Divorce

I am the Petitioner in this matter and I enclose:

Request for Bailiff Service

Cheque for £10 [unless you qualified for remission of Fees]

Recent photograph of the Respondent.

Thank you for your assistance in this matter.

Yours faithfully

Letter to Court asking for the Decree Nisi to be made Absolute

Your address

Date

Chief Clerk

.... County Court

[Address of County Court]

Case no: [if you have one, insert it here]

Dear Sir

Divorce

I am the Petitioner in this matter and I wish to apply for my Decree Nisi to be made Absolute. I enclose:

Application form

Cheque for £30 [unless you qualified for Remission of Fees]

Thank you for your assistance in this matter.

Yours faithfully

Useful Contacts

Replacement marriage certificates

There are two options:

1. Send for a copy from the local Registrar of Births, Deaths and Marriages, which will cost £6.50 and take about two weeks. If you want it urgently they can get a copy out to you by the next working day for £22.

2. Write to The Registrar General
   OPCS Southport
   Smedley Hydro
   Trafalgar Road
   Southport PR8 2HH.

   Send a cheque for £11 – or £27 if you require them to send you your copy within two working days– made out to HMPG together with details of your and your partner's full names, where you were married and the date.

Courts and official forms

Lord Chancellor's Department
54 Victoria Street
London SW1E 6QW
Tel 020 7210 8500
Fax 020 7210 8740
Email: >generalenquiries@lcdhq.gsi.gov.uk
Website: >www.opengov.uk/lcd<

On the website there is a list of courts in England and Wales which 'do' divorce and other family law matters. There are also examples of all the forms you are likely to need on the website but times, fees and forms do change and it is worth calling your local court to check whether or not there have been any changes. Or access >http://www.courtservice.gov.uk<

Housing and property matters

Land Registry
HM Land Registry
32 Lincoln's Inns Fields
London WC2A 3PH
Tel: 020 7917 8888
Fax: 020 7955 0110
Website: >www.landreg.gov.uk<

District Land Registry Offices

Birkenhead District Land Registry (1)
Titles in Cheshire, Kensington and Hammersmith
Rosebrae Court,
Woodside Ferry Approach
Birkenhead CH41 6DU
Tel: 0151 472 6666
Fax: 0151 472 6789

Birkenhead District Land Registry (2)
Titles in Merseyside and Staffordshire
Old Market House
Hamilton St
Birkenhead CH41 5FL
Tel: 0151 473 1110/1106
Fax: 0151 473 0251

Coventry District Land Registry
All titles
Leigh Court, Torrington Ave
Tile Hill
Coventry CV4 9XZ
Tel: 02476 860860/860864
Fax: 02476 860021

Croydon District Land Registry
All titles
Sunley House
Bedford Park
Croydon CR9 3LE

Tel: 020 8781 9100/9103
Fax: 020 8781 9110

District Land Registry for Wales (Corfrestrfa Tir Ddosbarthol Cymru)
Titles in Wales
Ty Cwm Tawe, Phoenix Way
Llansamlet
Swansea SA7 9FQ
Tel: 01792 355000
Fax: 01792 355055

Durham (Boldon House) District Land Registry (1)
Titles in Cumbria and Surrey
Boldon House
Wheatlands Way
Pity Me
Durham DH1 5GJ
Tel: 0191 301 2345
Fax: 0191 301 2300 DX: 60860 Durham 6

Durham (Southfield House) District Land Registry (2)
Titles in Cleveland, Durham Northumberland, and Tyne and Wear
Southfield House
Southfield Way
Durham DH1 5TR
Tel: 0191 301 3500
Fax: 0191 301 0020

Gloucester District Land Registry
All titles
Twyver House
Bruton way
Gloucester GL1 1DQ
Tel: 01452 511111
Fax: 01452 510050

Harrow District Land Registry
All titles
Lyon House
Lyon Road
Harrow HA1 2EU
Tel: 020 8235 1181
Fax: 020 8862 0176

Kingston upon Hull District Land Registry
All titles
Earle House
Portland Street
Kingston upon Hull HU2 8JN
Tel: 01482 223244
Fax: 01482 224278

Lancashire District Land Registry
All titles
Wrea Brook Court
Lytham Road
Warton
Preston PR4 1TE
Tel: 01772 836 700
Fax: 01772 836 970

Leicester District Land Registry
All titles
Westbridge Place
Leicester LE1 5DR
Tel: 0116 265 4000
Fax: 0116 265 4008

Lytham District Land Registry
All titles
Birkenhead House
East Beach
Lytham St Annes FY8 5AB
Tel: 01253 849849/840012
Fax: 01253 840001

Nottingham District Land Registry (1) (East)
Titles in South Yorkshire and Nottinghamshire
Robin's Wood Road
Nottingham NG8 3RQ
Tel: 0115 906 5353
Fax: 0115 936 0036

Nottingham District Land Registry (2) (West)
Titles in West Yorkshire and Derbyshire
Chalfont Drive
Nottingham NG8 3RN
Tel: 0115 935 1166
Fax: 0115 935 0038

Peterborough District Land Registry
All titles
Touthill Close
City Road
Peterborough PE1 1XN
Tel: 01733 288288
Fax: 01733 280022

Plymouth District Land Registry
All titles
Plumer House
Tailyour Road
Crownhill
Plymouth PL6 5HY
Tel: 01752 636000/636123
Fax: 01752 636161

Portsmouth District Land Registry
All titles
St Andrew's Court
St Michael's Road
Portsmouth PO1 2JH
Tel: 023 92768888
Fax: 023 92768768

Stevenage District Land Registry
All titles
Brickdale House
Swingate
Stevenage SG1 1XG
Tel: 01438 788888/788889
Fax: 01438 780107

Swansea District Land Registry
Titles in England
Ty Bryn Glas
High St
Swansea SA1 1PW
Tel: 01792 458877
Fax: 01792 473236

Telford District Land Registry
All titles
Parkside Court
Hall Park Way
Telford TF3 4LR
Tel: 01952 290355
Fax: 01952 290356

Tunbridge Wells District Land Registry
All titles
Forest Court
Forest Rd
Tunbridge Wells TN2 5AQ
Tel: 01892 510015
Fax: 01892 510032

Wales *(see District Land Registry for Wales)*

Weymouth District Land Registry
All titles
Melcombe Court
1 Cumberland Drive
Weymouth DT4 9TT
Tel: 01305 363636
Fax: 01305 363646

York District Land Registry
All titles
James House
James Street
York YO1 3YZ
Tel: 01904 450000
Fax: 01904 450086

Land Charges Department
Land Registry Plymouth
Drake's Hill Court
Burrington Way
Plymouth PL5 3LP
Tel: 01752 635600
Telephone searches: 01752 635635
Fax: 01752 766666

Telephone Outline Applications
England: 0845 308 4545
Wales: 0845 307 4535

Housing Benefit
Your local council will have all the leaflets about Housing Benefit, but you can also access:

Affordable and low income housing
A website listing housing associations >http://uk.dir.yahoo.com/Society< will get you there.

Women's Link
Women's Housing Advice in London. 'A free and confidential advisory service offering support and advocacy as well as a comprehensive information service, for all low-income women in London'. Access >http://212.53.89.136/wlink<

Council of Mortgage Lenders
3 Savile Row
London W1X 1AF
Information telephone line: 020 7440 2255
Website: >www.eml.org.uk<

Ask for their useful free fact sheet *Assistance with Mortgage Payments.*

Shelter National Campaign for the Homeless
88 Old Street
London EC1V 9HU
Helpline: 0808 800 4444 (24 hours)
Website: >www.shelter.org.uk<

Lawyers

See also Solicitor's Family Law Association

Law Society of England and Wales
113 Chancery Lane
London WC2 1PL
Tel: 020 7242 1222

Office for the Supervision of Solicitors
Victoria Court
8 Dormer Place
Leamington Spa
Warwickshire CV32 5AE
Helpline: 08456 086 6565
Enquiry desk tel: 01926 820082

Income Support and other benefits

Department of Social Security (DSS) (but see below)
Tel: 020 7712 2171
Fax: 020 7712 2386

(but see your local telephone directory for offices near you).

The newly (at the time of writing) renamed Department for Work and Pensions offers a website, >http://www.dss.gov.uk< that gives details of all benefits, as well as links with other useful benefit-related sites. You could, at the time of writing, still get the old DSS site on the same address.

Disability Working Allowance Unit
Inland Revenue
PO Box 178
Preston PR1 0YY
Tel: 08456 055858
Fax: 01772 239794
Minicom: 08456 088844

Legal Help and Public Funding

Community Legal Service
Selborne House
54–60 Victoria Street
London SW1A 6QW
Tel: 08456 081122
Website: >www.justask.org.uk<

Children and the family

Solicitors' Family Law Association
366 Crofton Road
Farnborough
Orpington
Kent BR6 8NN
Tel: 01689 850227
Fax: 01689 855833

An association of over 5,000 solicitors that are 'committed to promoting a non-confrontational atmosphere in which family law matters are dealt with in a sensitive, constructive and cost-effective way'. Click on the SFLA website >http://www.sfla.co.uk< for details of SFLA solicitors near you.

Child Support Agency (CSA)
The CSA provides two helplines:
For information telephone: 0345 830830.
For forms telephone: 0345 134134.
Otherwise, there are branches in main DSS offices.

The CSA also has a website, >http://www.dss.gov.uk/csa< that can also be accessed through the DSS site (see above).

Child Support Practitioners' Group
c/o James Pirrie
The Family Law Consortium
2 Henrietta Street
London WC2E 8PS
Email: >jp@tflc.co.uk<

A group of about 200 solicitors who major in legal problems relating to the CSA. They can often direct you to a member near you.

NSPCC – if children are in danger the NSPCC has a free 24-hour national link line: 0808 800 5000
Website: >http://www.nspcc.org.uk<

Parentline Plus
520 Highgate Studios
53–79 Highgate Road
Kentish Town
London NW5 1TL
Tel: 0808 800 2222
Website: >www.parentline.co.uk<

Families Need Fathers
'Keeping Children and Parents in Contact Since 1974'
134 Curtain Road
London EC2A 3AR
Tel: 0207 613 5060

Go to its website >http://www.fnf.org.uk< for much useful information, including the *Rough Guide to Law.*

Gingerbread
'The leading support organisation for lone parent families in England and Wales'.

Advice and support groups, and also produces *Lone Parents' Handbook.*

7 Sovereign Court
Sovereign Close
London E1W 3HW
Tel: 020 7488 9300
Fax: 020 7488 9333
E-mail: office@gingerbread.org.uk
Free advice line: 0800 018 4318 (10 a.m.– 4 p.m. Monday to Friday)
Website: >http://www.gingerbread.org.uk<

Grandparents' Federation
Moot House
The Stow
Harlow
Essex CM20 3AG
Helpline: 02179 444964

Advice, support and information for grandparents of children affected by family break-up.

Emergency help

Police – usually listed in your telephone directory under Police.

Social Services – usually listed under the name of your local authority, eg Suffolk County Council.

Local housing departments – listed with your local council.

Women's Aid Federation
'Working to end violence against women and children'. Advice, support and temporary accommodation for women and children fleeing domestic violence.
National helpline: 0845 702 3468.
Website: >http://womensaid.org.uk<

London Rape Crisis Centre
Tel: 020 7837 1600

Marriage guidance, mediation and other counselling

Relate

'We provide counselling, sex therapy, relationship education and training to support couple and family relationships throughout life.'

Relate
Herbert Gray College
Little Church Street
Rugby
Warwickshire CV21 3AP
Tel: 01788 573241

There are nearly 100 Relate centres in England, Wales and Northern Ireland with 2,500 trained counsellors. Look in your local telephone directory under Relate, or access its website, >http://www.relate.org.uk< which offers useful links with other organisations – access >http://www.relate.org.uk/links.htm< and go to the organisation you want. These include:

UK College of Family Mediators
24–32 Stephenson Way
London NW1 2HX
Tel: 020 7391 9162
Fax: 020 7391 9165
Website: >www.ukcfm.co.uk<

Websites linked to the Relate website

National Family Mediation

NFM is a network of over 60 local not-for-profit Family Mediation Services in England and Wales, offering help to couples who are in the process of separating or divorcing.

WPF (Westminster Pastoral Foundation)

General counselling services in the UK with over 30 years' experience of helping people in all kinds of distress.

Home-Start

Provides support, friendship and practical help to families with at least one child under five.

One Plus One

Monitors contemporary marriages and relationships, focusing on understanding the causes, effects and prevention of relationship breakdown.

National Family and Parenting Institute

An independent charity to provide a strong national focus on parenting and families in the 21st century.

Other Useful Helplines

African Caribbean Family Mediation Service
Tel: 020 7738 6090

Asian Family Counselling Service
Tel: 020 8997 5749 and 020 8967 5390

Family Crisis Line
Tel: 01483 722533

National Council for Divorced and Separated
Tel: 0114 231 3585

National Council for One Parent Families
Tel: 020 7428 5420

National Association of Citizen's Advice Bureaux
http://nacab.uk

And finally, access >www.divorce.co.uk<

Index